MIND BREATHS

Poems 1972-1977

ALLEN GINSBERG

"Time after time for such a journey none but iron pens
Can write And adamantine leaves receive nor can the man who goes
The journey obstinate refuse to write time after time"

— Wm. Blake

CITY LIGHTS BOOKS
San Francisco

First printing: January 1978
Second printing: June 1978

Diligent readers will find 22 additional Poems rhymed, many with music notation, Published as *First Blues: Rags, Ballads & Harmonium Songs 1971-1974,* Full Court Press, N.Y. 1975, to correlate with *Mind Breaths,* supplementing the volume of musical inspiration.

Library of Congress Cataloging in Publication Data:

Ginsberg, Allen, 1926-
    Mind breaths.

    (Pocket poets series; no. 35)
    I.   Title.   II.   Series.
PS3513.174M5   811'.5'4   77-541
ISBN: 0-87286-101-5 (cloth)
ISBN: 0-87286-092-2 (paper)

CITY LIGHTS BOOKS are edited by Lawrence Ferlinghetti & Nancy J. Peters, and published at the City Lights Bookstore, Columbus & Broadway, San Francisco, California 94133.

dedicated to

Vajra Acharya

Chögyam Trungpa, Rinpoche

Poet

"Guru Death your words are true
Teacher Death I do thank you
For inspiring me to sing this Blues"

ACKNOWLEDGMENTS

This half-decade of poems was first printed in River Styx, Bastard Angel, Chicago, Georgia Strait, Vancouver Express, Lama Foundation: Bountiful Lord's Delivery Service, Berkeley Barb, New Departures, The Villager, Transatlantic Review, Lowenfel's Anthology, The American Pen International Quarterly, Rolling Stone, Peninsula Skyway, Gay Sunshine Los Angeles Times, New York Times, W.I.N. Magazine, Bad Breath, Stupa: Naropa Student Newsletter, Bombay Gin, Red Osier Press, A Hundred Posters, Title I, Brahma, The Workingman's Press, The End Magazine, Chicago Review, New Directions Annual, New Age Journal, Allen Verbatim (ed. Gordon Ball, McGraw-Hill), Painted Bride Quarterly, Seven Days, Expresso, Jack Albert's Boston Newspaper, Loka, College Press Service, Rolling Thunder Review Phantom Newsletter, Folger Shakespeare Library Broadside, Soho News, A Shout in the Streets, City Lights Anthology, Stone Press Weekly, Unspeakable Visions of the Individual.

Calligraphy *AH* by Chögyam Trungpa, Rinpoche
Wheel of Life, Tibet: Collection of the Newark Museum

Tag lines for "Returning to the Country for a Brief Visit" are from *Moments of Rising Mist, a Collection of Sung Landscape Poetry*, Mushinsha/Grossman, 1973.

Final typescript was assembled at Jack Kerouac School of Disembodied Poetics, Naropa Institute, Boulder, Colorado. Arthur Russell and Brian Muney transcribed song music by the author.

CONTENTS

AYERS ROCK ULURU SONG

When the red pond fills fish appear

When the red pond dries fish disappear.

Everything built on the desert crumbles to dust.

Electric cable transmission wires swept down.

The lizard people came out of the rock.

The red Kangaroo people forgot their own song.

Only a man with four sticks can cross the Simpson Desert.

One rain turns red dust green with leaves.

One raindrop begins the universe.

When the raindrop dries, worlds come to their end.

Central Australia
23 March 1972

XMAS GIFT

I met Einstein in a dream
Springtime on Princeton lawn grass
I kneeled down & kissed his young thumb
like a ruddy pope
his face fresh broad cheeked rosy
"I invented a universe separate,
something like a Virgin"—
"Yes, the creature gives birth to itself,"
I quoted from Mescaline
We sat down open air universal summer
to eat lunch, professors' wives
at the Tennis Court Club,
our meeting eternal, as expected,
my gesture to kiss his fist
unexpectedly saintly
considering the Atom Bomb I didn't mention.

24 December 1972

THOUGHTS SITTING BREATHING

OM — the pride of perfumed money, music food from
      China, a place to sit quiet

MA — How jealous! the million Pentagon myrmidons with
      dollar billions to spend on Rock & Roll, restaurant
      high thrones in sky filled with Electric Bombers — Ah!
      how jealous they are of the thin stomached Vietnamese
      boy.

NI — Lust in heart for the pink tender prick'd school-boy up-
      stairs bedroom naked with his books, high school
      locker shower, stretching on the bed, the young
      guitar player's ass

PA — Impercipience, cat meows natural words at the window,
      dog barks cheerful morn, cockroach feelers touch the
      wall, the fly buzzes long long on the sunny windowsill
      lying upside-down in deathly prayer exhausted, man
      bends over oblivious books, buds stick forth their
      heart-tips when ice melts New Year's eve, green grass
      shoots show 'neath melted snow, screams rise out of
      thousands of mouths in Hanoi —

DMI — alone the misery, the broken legs of carcrash alcohol,
      gimme another cigarette, I ain't got a dime for coffee,
      got no rupee for rice ain't got no land I got hunger in
      my gland my belly's swollen potatoes my knees got
      cut on the Tanks —

HŪM — the pigs got rocks in their head, C.I.A. got one eye
      bloody mind tongue, fiends sold my phonograph TV
      set to the junkman, Hate that dog shat my rug, hate

Wheel of Life

Gook Heaven, hate them hippies in Hell stinking
Marijuana smog city.

OM — Give it all away, poetry bliss & ready cash for taxicabs,
walk Central Park alone & cook your beans in empty
silence watching the Worm crawl thru meat walls —
MA — sit down crosslegged and relax, storm Heaven with
your mental guns? Give up let Angels alone to play
their guitars in Hollywood and drink their Coke-
snuff in mountainside bathroom peace —
NI — Light as ashes, love for Neal sublimed into Poesy, love
for Peter gone into the Vegetable garden to grow
corn & tomatoes —
PA — Dog bark! call the mind gods! scream happiness in
Saigon behind the bar my mother in throes of Police
vomit rape! that garbage can I threw in Atlantic
Ocean floats over Father Fisheye's sacred grave —
DMI — I forgive thee Cord Meyer secret mind police suborned
the Student Congress Cultural Freedom & destroyed
Intellect in Academe Columbia Harvard made great
murder Indochina War our fantasy-bomb gutted
New York's soul —
HŪM — Miserable victims flashing knives, Hell's Angels
Manson Nixon Calley-Ma, all the cops in the world
and their gangster lovers, car salesmen Wall Street
brokers smoking in rage over dwindling oil supplies,
O poor sick junkies all here's bliss of Buddha-opium,
Sacred Emptiness to fix your angry brains —

OM — the Crown of Emptiness, relax the skullcap wove of
formal thought, let light escape to Heaven, floating
up from heart thru cranium, free space for Causeless
Bliss —

MA — Speech purified, worlds calmed of alcoholic luxury &
irritable smoking, jealous fucking rush thru taxicab
cities, mental cancer pig war fever machines — Heart
through throat, free space for Causeless Bliss!

NI — How vast, how brightly empty and how old, the breath
within the breast expands threefold, the sigh of no
restraint, sigh love's release, the rest and peacefulness
of sweethearts' ease, from Heart to Heart — free space
for Causeless Bliss!

PA — Dog bellies crying happy in the snow, worms share
mind's heaviest part, elephants carry Angels whose
animal trumpets blow from abdomen deep navel up
into the heart — free space for Causeless Bliss

DMI — Down in the pecker, the empty piece of wood — Every-
one I fucked is dead and gone — everyone I'm gonna
fuck is turning to a ghost — All my penis blessedness
never'll get lost, but rise from loins & come in my
heart — free space for Causeless Bliss

HŪM — I shit out my hate thru my asshole, My sphincter
loosens the void, all hell's legions fall thru space, the
Pentagon is destroyed

> United States armies march thru the past
> The Chinese legions rage
> Past the Great Wall of Maya
> And scream on the central stage

MARCH: THOUGHTS SITTING BREATHING

C   F

I shit out my hate thru my asshole, My sphincter

loosens the void, all hell's legions fall thru space
G

The Pentagon is destroyed   United States Armies march
F   C

thru the Past   The Chinese legions rage Past the
F

Great Wall of Maya and scream on the Central Stage
C   F

I loose my bowels of Asia   I move the U.S.A.
C   G

I crap on Dharmakaya   And wipe the worlds away
C

White House filled with Fuel-gas bombs ... etc   1-4-1-5

Allen Ginsberg   Musick'd May 1977
S.F.

8

I loose my bowels of Asia,
I move the U.S.A.
I crap on Dharmakaya
And wipe the worlds away
White House filled with fuel gas bombs
Slums with rats' faeces & teeth
All Space is fore-given to Emptiness—
From earth to heart, free space
                    for Causeless Bliss

January 1, 1973

"WHAT WOULD YOU DO IF YOU LOST IT?"

said Rinpoche Chögyam Trungpa Tulku in the marble glit-
     tering apartment lobby
looking at my black hand-box full of Art, "Better prepare for
     Death". . .
The harmonium that's Peter's
the scarf that's Krishna's the bell and brass lightningbolt Phil
     Whalen selected in Japan
a tattered copy of Blake, with chord notations, black books
     from City Lights,
Australian Aborigine song sticks, green temple incense,
     Tibetan precious-metal finger cymbals—
A broken leg a week later enough reminder, lay in bed and
     after few days' pain began to weep
no reason, thinking a little of Rabbi Schacter, a little of father
     Louis, a little
of everything that must be abandoned,
snow abandoned,
empty dog barks after the dogs have disappeared
meals eaten passed thru the body to nourish tomatoes and
     corn,
The wooden bowl from Haiti too huge for my salad,
Teachings, Tantras, Haggadahs, Zohar, Revelations, poet-
     ries, Koans
forgotten with the snowy world, forgotten
with generations of icicles crashing to white gullies by
     roadside,
Dharmakaya forgot, Nirmanakaya shoved in coffin, Sambho-

gakaya eclipsed in candle-light snuffed by the playful cat—

Goodbye my own treasures, bodies adored to the nipple,

old souls worshipped flower-eye or imaginary auditory panoramic skull—

goodbye old socks washed over & over, blue boxer shorts, subzero longies,

new Ball Boots black hiplength for snowdrifts near the farm mailbox,

goodbye to my room full of books, all wisdoms I never studied, all the Campion, Creeley, Anacreon Blake I never read through,

blankets farewell, orange diamonded trunked from Mexico for tearful age, Himalayan sheepwool lugged down from Almora days with Lama Govinda and Peter trying to eat tough stubborn halfcooked chicken.

Paintings on wall, Maitreya, Sakyamuni & Padmasambhava, Dr. Samedi with Haitian spats & cane whiskey,

Bhaktivedanta Swami at desk staring sad eye Krishna at my hopeless selfconsciousness,

Attic full of toys, desk full of old checks, files on NY police & C.I.A. peddling Heroin,

Files on laughing Leary, files on Police State, files on ecosystems all faded & brown,

notebooks untranscribed, hundreds of little poems & prose my own hand,

newspaper interviews, assemblaged archives, useless paperworks surrounding me imperfectly chronologic, humorous later in eternity, reflective of Cities' particular streets studios and boudoirs—

goodbye poetry books, I don't have to take you along
anymore on a chain to Deux Magots like a red lobster
thru Paris, Moscow, Prague, Milan, New York, Calcutta,
Bangkok, holy Benares, yea Rishikesh & Brindaban may
yr prana lift ye over the roof of the world—
my own breath slower now, silent waiting & watching—
Downstairs pump-organs, musics, rags and blues, home made
Blake hymns, mantras to raise the skull of America,
goodbye C chord, F chord, G chord, goodbye all the chords
of The House of the Rising Sun
Goodbye farmhouse, city apartment, garbage subways Empire
State, Museum of Modern Art where I wandered thru
puberty dazzled by Van Gogh's raw-brained star-systems
pasted on blue thick skyey Suchness—
Goodbye again Naomi, goodbye old painful legged poet
Louis, goodbye Paterson the 69 between Joe Bozzo &
Harry Haines that out-lasted childhood & poisoned the
air o'er Passaic Valley,
goodbye Broadway, give my regards to the great falls & boys
staring marijuana'd in wonder at the quiet roar of God-
father Williams' speech
Goodbye old poets of Century that taught fixed eye & sharp
tongue from Pound with silent Mouni heart to Tom
Veitch weeping in Stinson Beach,
goodbye to my brothers who write poetry & play fiddle, my
nephews who blow tuba & stroke bass viol, whistle flute
or smile & sing in blue rhythm,
goodbye shades of dead living loves, bodies weeping bodies
broken bodies aging, bodies turned to wax doll or
cinder

Goodbye America you hope you prayer you tenderness, you
   IBM 135-35 Electronic Automated Battlefield Igloo White
   Dragon-tooth Fuel-Air Bomb over Indochina

Goodbye Heaven, farewell Nirvana, sad Paradise adieu,
   adios all angels and archangels, devas & devakis, Bodhi-
   sattvas, Buddhas, rings of Seraphim, Constellations of
   elect souls weeping singing in the golden Bhumi Rungs,
   goodbye High Throne, High Central Place, Alleluiah
   Light beyond Light, a wave of the hand to Thee Central
   Golden Rose,

Om Ah Hūṁ A La La Ho Sophia, Soham Tara Ma, Om Phat
   Svaha Padmasambhava Marpa Mila sGam.po.pa Kar-
   mapa Trungpaye! Namastaji Brahma, Ave atque vale
   Eros, Jupiter, Zeus, Apollo, Surya, Indra

Bom Bom! Shivaye!   Ram Nam Satyahey! Om Ganipatti,
   Om Saraswati Hrih Sowha! Ardinarishvara Radha Hare-
   krishna faretheewell forevermore!

None left standing! No tears left for eyes, no eyes for weeping,
   no mouth for singing, no song for the hearer, no more
   words for any mind.

February 1, 1973

YES AND IT'S HOPELESS

hundred million cars running out of gasoline
million coalstoves burning shale carbonmist over cities
Hopeless I'll never get laid again, O what a beautiful body
    that boy from Jersey City last night
Hopeless, locked in plaster-of-Paris leg cast, bones, skull
    heart, intestines, liver, eyes and tongue
All hopeless, the entire solar system running Thermody-
    namics' Second Law
down the whole galaxy, all universes brain illusion or solid
    electric hopeless emptiness
evacuating itself through quasar pressure Furnaces,
hopeless the 300,000 junkies in N.Y.
hopeless President waging war, "fighting for peace" sending
    State Secretary to Israel, the moon, China, Acapulco,
hopeless the Dutch boy standing with his finger in the dyke,
the energy crisis, the protein crisis 1990, the Folklore Crisis,
    the Aboriginal Crisis, the Honkie Crisis, the old Nazi
    Crisis, the Arab Crisis, the Chrysophrase Crisis, Tung-
    sten, the crisis in Panama, Brazil, Uruguay, Argentina,
    Chile, Peru, Bolivia, Venezuela, Santo Domingo, Haiti,
    Cuba, Florida, Alabama, Texas, New Jersey, New York,
    East 10th Street, the Crisis in San Juan Capistrano, the
    Oil-spill in Bolinas Bay, Santa Barbara's tar tide, the crisis
    of the Loch Ness Monster & the Dublin Bomb Crisis,
all hopeless, the overpopulation of dogs, humans, cock-
    roaches, rats, Crown of Thorn Starfish, green algae in
    Lake Erie —

Hopeless, hopeless, Jesus on the Cross or Buddha voided
passing through

Hopeless, the First Zen Institute, the Second Church of the
Resurrection, The Third Eye System Inc., the 4th Estate,
the 5th Column in the Kundalini, the 6th sense, the Sev-
enth Seal Chowder & Marching Society the 8th Nerve
in the Vagus Nebula System the 9th Degree Samadhi
Monopoly the 10th sorry passenger on the bus crashed
over Freeway's iron ropes down into the Swamp Abyss
outsida Roanoke—

OK hopeless, Rolling Stone Consciousness, mammoth Sun-
day NY Times

Hopeless all silence, all Yoga, all quiet Ecstasies of Saints and
Starvation Monks Ceylon to Bhutan—

Hopeless two million deaths in Indochina, the half million
Communists assassinated in Indonesia? Slaughter of
Innocents in Mexico City, Massacres of Wounded Knee
My-Lai Lidice Attica, 15 million never came back from
Siberia

the jail murder of George Jackson, Sacco & Vanzetti electro-
cuted Rosenbergs, bullet assassination of Kennedy,
Luther King, Malcolm X, the burning of Zwingli,
hemlock death of Socrates the headless catastrophe
Jayne Mansfield's autocrash & Jimmy Dean's highway
wreckaged body—

Hopeless, the poems of Dante & Shakespeare, such stuff as
dreams are made of, Burroughs' Orwell systems, Spengler
& Vico's cycles, Padmasambhava Krishnamurti—empty,
hopeless

as the great oilfields of Persia
reservoirs of petrochemicals under Alaskan permafrost &
    Indochinese ocean wave
petroleum cracker tanks in Venezuela & robot pumps of Los
    Angeles,
brokendown cars on the farm, the tire-less Ford,
Oldsmobile sans batteries, dead corpse of Myron the neighbor
    Farmer the live corpse of Ginsberg the prophet
Hopeless.

March 10, 1973

UNDER THE WORLD THERE'S A LOT OF ASS, A LOT OF CUNT

a lot of mouths and cocks,
under the world there's a lot of come, and a lot of saliva drip-
    ping into brooks,
There's a lot of Shit under the world, flowing beneath cities
    into rivers,
a lot of urine floating under the world,
a lot of snot in the world's industrial nostrils, sweat under the
    world's iron arm, blood
gushing out of the world's breast,
endless lakes of tears, seas of sick vomit rushing between hemi-
    spheres
floating toward Sargasso, old oily rags and brake fluids,
    human gasoline—
Under the world there's pain, fractured thighs, napalm burn-
    ing in black hair, phosphorus eating elbows to bone
insecticides contaminating oceantide, plastic dolls floating
    across Atlantic,
Toy soldiers crowding the Pacific, B-52 bombers choking
    jungle air with vaportrails and brilliant flares
Robot drones careening over rice terraces dropping cluster
    grenades, plaster pellets spray into flesh, dragontooth
    mines & jellied fires fall on straw roofs and water buffalos,
perforating village huts with barbed shrapnel, trenchpits
    filled with fuel-gas-poison'd explosive powders—

Under the world there's broken skulls, crushed feet, cut eye-
    balls, severed fingers, slashed jaws,
Dysentery, homeless millions, tortured hearts, empty souls.

April 1973

RETURNING TO THE COUNTRY
FOR A BRIEF VISIT

(Annotations to Amitendranath Tagore's Sung Poetry)

"In later days, remembering this I shall certainly go mad."

Reading Sung poems, I think of my poems to Neal
dead few years now, Jack underground
invisible—their faces rise in my mind.
Did I write truthfully of them? In later times
I saw them little, not much difference they're dead.
They live in books and memory, strong as on earth.

*"Do not wait for youth, for it passes
like a gust of wind."*

The old small dog trembles in April sunlight
on winter-brown grass. Snow gone, so youth
is gone, though this sunlight shines
on naked bodies West one more spring.
A redwing whistles, flying over the pine tree.

"My host's table is heaped with official work.
He returns to it morning and evening,
And now there is a touch of white in his hair."

Sitting in the frontyard; chickadees chirk chirk chirk
from sunlit treetops, maples lift bare arms
under blue sky. Typewriter and paper
sit on the table indoors, empty. I roll down
overalls, take off my shirt,
the dog falls on his side in the grass, sighing.

"May I inquire of the mountain folks,
Where is that cloud now?"

Not one cloud in the sky
no noise but wind in State pinewoods.
Old floppy straw hat, middleaged & alone.
Black cat walks down the road meowing.

"I do not know who is hoarding all this rare work."

Old One the dog stretches stiff legged,
soon he'll be underground. Spring's first fat bee
buzzes yellow over the new grass and dead leaves.

What's this little brown insect walking zigzag
across the sunny white page of Su Tung-p'o's poem?
Fly away, tiny mite, even your life is tender —
I lift the book and blow you into the dazzling void.

"I fear that others may know I am here;
An immortal may appear to welcome me."

Right leg broken, can't walk around
visit the fishpond to touch the cold water,
tramp thru willows to the lonely meadow across the brook—
here comes a metal landrover, brakes creaking hello.

"You live apart on rivers and seas . . ."

You live in apartments by rivers and seas
Spring comes, waters flow murky, the salt wave's covered
    with oily dung
Sun rises, smokestacks cover the roofs with black mist
winds blow, city skies are clear blue all afternoon
but at night the full moon hesitates behind brick.
How will all these millions of people worship the Great
    Mother?
When all these millions of people die, will they recognize
    the Great Father?

"I always remember the year I made it over the mountain pass."

Robins and sparrows warble in mild spring dusk
sun sets behind green pines in the little valley
High over my roof grey branches sway gently under motion-
    less clouds
Hunters guns sounded three times in the hillside aspen
The house sat silent as I looked above my book,
quiet old poems about the Yi & Tsangpo Rivers—
I always remember the spring I climbed Glacier Peak with Gary.

*"Can we not avoid wordly scholars
And refine ourselves with that mysterious essence?*

Setting sun shines in the pond below
our rusty barn and falls behind a hill.
The radio in the house echoes scandals in the Capital!
Robins, bluejays crows and chickadees cry louder
as the sun turns orange. A bad leg stays me
out in the garden, my head under the clouds.
Girls shout by the appletree, dogs bark at the red sky.

April 20, 1973

NIGHT GLEAM

Over and over thru the dull material world the call is made
over and over thru the dull material world I make the call
O English folk, in Sussex night, thru black beech tree branches
the full moon shone at three AM, I stood in under wear on
    the lawn—
I saw a mustached English man I loved, with athlete's breast
    and farmer's arms,
I lay in bed that night   many loves beating in my heart
sleepless hearing songs of generations electric returning in-
    telligent memory
to my frame, and so went to dwell again in my heart
and worship the Lovers there, love's teachers, youths and
    poets who live forever
in the secret heart, in the dark night, in the full moon, year
    after year
over & over thru the dull material world the call is made.

16 July 1973

WHAT I'D LIKE TO DO

Retire abandon world sd Swami Bhaktivedanta my age 47 approaching half-century

Go to San Marino see Blake's vision of Moloch, go to Manchester see Moloch

Visit Blake's works all over World West, study prophetic Books interpret Blake unify Vision

Step in same river twice

Build hermitage of wood and stone with porch 3000 foot up Rockies, Sierras, Catskills fine soft forests

sit crosslegged straight spine belly relaxed heart humming Ah each exhalation

Inspiration established compose English Apocalypse American science Greek rhythm Tibetan mantra Blues

long hours half-lotus-legged at desk window pine trees omming in rainy wind

Spend three years in solitude Naropa's Six Doctrines mastered and another hundred days intermediate State twixt Death and Birth

Read Milton's Paradise Lost decipher Egyptian Book of Dead and Annutara Tantra etc.

Compose poems to the wind

Chant into electric microphones, pacify Rock, enrich

skull emptiness with vocal salami taxicabs, magnetize nervous systems,

destroy Empire State's dead Life Time smog

Masturbate in peace, haunt ancient cities for boys, practice
  years of chastity, save Jewels for God my own ruddy
  body, hairy delicate antennae
Vegetable, eat carrots, fork cabbage, spoon peas, fry potatoes,
  boil beets, ox forgiven, pig forgotten, hot dogs ban-
  ished from celestial realms cloud-roofed over Kitkitdizze's
  green spring weeds—milk, angel-Milk
Read Dostoyevsky's Brothers Karamazov I lay down half-
  finished a dozen times decades ago
Compose last choirs of Innocence & Experience, set music to
  tongues of Rossetti Mss. orchestrate Jerusalem's qua-
  trains—
War's over, soft mat wood floor, flower vase on inkstand, blue
  oaks gazing in the window.

August 1973 London

ON NERUDA'S DEATH

Some breath breathes out *Adonais* & *Canto General*
Some breath breathes out Bombs and dog barks
Some breath breathes silent over green snow mountains
Some breath breathes not at all

25 Sept 1973

MIND BREATHS

Thus crosslegged on round pillow sat in Teton Space—
I breathed upon the aluminum microphone-stand a body's
    length away
I breathed upon the teacher's throne, the wooden chair with
    yellow pillow
I breathed further, past the sake cup half emptied by the
    breathing guru
Breathed upon the green sprigged thick-leaved plant in a
    flowerpot
Breathed upon the vast plateglass shining back th' assembled
    sitting Sangha in the meditation cafeteria
my breath thru nostril floated out to the moth of evening
    beating into window'd illumination
breathed outward over aspen twigs trembling September's
    top yellow leaves twilit at mountain foot
breathed over the mountain, over snowpowdered crags ringed
    under slow-breathed cloud-mass white spumes
windy across Tetons to Idaho, grey ranges under blue space
    swept
with delicate snow flurries, breaths Westward
mountain grass trembling in tiny winds toward Wasatch
Breezes south late autumn in Salt Lake's temple wooden
    streets,
white salt dust lifted swirling by the thick leaden lake, dust
    carried up over Kennicot's pit onto the massive Unit Rig,
out towards Reno's neon, dollar bills skittering downstreet
    along the curb,

up into Sierras oak leaves blown down by fall cold chills
over peaktops snowy gales beginning,
a breath of prayer down on Kitkitdizze's horngreen leaves
    close to ground,
over Gary's tile roof, over temple pillar, tents and manzanita
    arbors in Sierra pine foothills—
a breath falls over Sacramento Valley, roar of wind down the
    sixlane freeway across Bay Bridge

uproar of papers floating over Montgomery Street, pigeons
    flutter down before sunset from Washington Park's white
    churchsteeple—
Golden Gate waters whitecapped scudding out to Pacific
    spreads
over Hawaii a balmy wind thru Hotel palmtrees, a moist
    warmth swept over the airbase, a dank breeze in Guam's
    rotten Customs shed,
clear winds breathe on Fiji's palm & coral shores, by wooden
    hotels in Suva flags flutter, taxis whoosh by Friday
    night's black promenaders under the rock & roll disco-
    theque window upstairs beating with English neon—
on a breeze into Sydney, and across hillside grass where
    mushrooms lie low on Cow-Flops in Queensland, down
    Adelaide's alleys a flutter of music from Brian Moore's
    Dobro carried in the wind—
up thru Darwin Land, out Gove Peninsula green ocean
    breeze, clack of Yerkalla village song sticks by the trem-
    bling wave
Yea and a wind over mercurial waters of Japan North East, a
    hollow wooden gong echoes in Kyoto's temple hall below
    the graveyard's wavy grass

A foghorn blowing in the China Sea, torrential rains over Saigon, bombers float over Cambodia, visioned tiny from stone Avalokiteshvara's many-faced towers Angkor Wat in windy night,

a puff of opium out of a mouth yellowed in Bangkok, a puff of hashish flowing thick out of a bearded saddhu's nostrils & eyes in Nimtallah Burning Ghat,

wood smoke flowing in wind across Hoogley Bridge, incense wafted under the Bo Tree in Bodh Gaya, in Benares woodpiles burn at Manikarnika returning incensed souls to Shiva,

wind dallies in the amorous leaves of Brindaban, still air on the vast mosque floor above Old Delhi's alleyways,

wind blowing over Kausani town's stone wall, Himalayan peaktops ranged hundreds of miles along snowy horizon, prayer flags flutter over Almora's wood brown house-tops,

trade winds carry dhows thru Indian Ocean to Mombassa or down to Dar 'Sallam's riverside sail port, palms sway & sailors wrapped in cotton sleep on log decks—

Soft breezes up thru Red Sea to Elat's dry hotels, paper leaflets scatter by the Wailing Wall, drifting into the Sepulchre

Mediterranean zephyrs leaving Tel Aviv, over Crete, Lassithi Plains' windmills still turn the centuries near Zeus' birth cave

Piraeus wave-lashed, Venice lagoon's waters blown up over the floor of San Marco, Piazza flooded and mud on the marble porch, gondolas bobbing up & down choppy waters at the Zatteree,

chill September fluttering thru Milan's Arcade, cold bones &
overcoats flapping in St. Peter's Square,

down Appian Way silence by gravesites, stelae stolid on a
lonely grass path, the breath of an old man laboring up
road—

Across Scylla & Charybdis, Sicilian tobacco smoke wafted
across the boat deck,

into Marseilles coalstacks black fumes float into clouds,
steamer's white driftspume down wind all the way to
Tangier,

a breath of red-tinged Autumn in Provence, boats slow on
the Seine, the lady wraps her cloak tight round her
bodice on toppa Eiffel Tower's iron head—

across the Channel rough black-green waves, in London's
Piccadilly beercans roll on concrete neath Eros' silver
breast, the Sunday Times lifts and settles on wet fountain
steps—

over Iona Isle blue day and balmy Inner Hebrides breeze, fog
drifts across Atlantic,

Labrador white frozen blowing cold, down New York's can-
yons manila paper bags scurry toward Wall from Lower
East side—

a breath over my Father's head in his apartment on Park
Avenue Paterson,

a cold September breeze down from East Hill, Cherry
Valley's maples tremble red,

out thru Chicago Windy City the vast breath of Consciousness
dissolves, smokestacks and autos drift expensive fumes
ribboned across railroad tracks,

Westward, a single breath blows across the plains, Nebraska's
    fields harvested & stubble bending delicate in evening
    airs
up Rockies, from Denver's Cherry Creekbed another zephyr
    risen,
across Pike's Peak an icy blast at sunset, Wind River peaktops
    flowing toward the Tetons,
a breath returns vast gliding grass flats cow-dotted into Jack-
    son Hole, into a corner of the plains,
up the asphalt road and mud parking lot, a breeze of restless
    September, up wood stairways in the wind
into the cafeteria at Teton Village under the red tram lift
a calm breath, a silent breath, a slow breath breathes outward
    from the nostrils.

28 Sept 73

FLYING ELEGY

Denver tower blocks group'd under grey haze
on tracted plains gassed to azure horizon—
                                    —"no place to take revenge."
Alan Watts epicure drank much
sang bass Christo voice a long long long breathed Aum
      passed on
in sleep exhausted heart philosopher
wandering age 58 in Chinese dressing gown to seek for love,
      or enter Buddha blind
like this blue sky wing plunged thru rainbow halo in clouds'
      drifty whiteness
The skandas are a veil suchlike, no place to take revenge
Blessed the dead who can't fight back resent a poem knife or
      thought
Blessed the dead in ignorance, dead with no sores or cigarette
      yen
Blessed the dead that don't get laid, don't eat fine casseroles
      herb-spiced with crusty cheese
don't drink slow tea
don't waste petrol surveying clouds in Heaven
don't waste words at their condition, no one to talk to
Bless the free dead lecturing in the deep with moveless
      tongue
perfect meditators without thought, accomplished in Sunyatā
Bless the dead last Philosophers, thought of the thought of
      Philosophers
Perfected Wisdom's teachers escaped from Blessing and the
      Bliss of grasping prayer

'scaped from the curse of meditation on a cushion on yr ass
Dead that've left breath, renounced sex body, suffered stroke
    & begone
alone, the drinker, thinker, divorcé, grandfather weary wise
dying in bed night's stillness silent and wake.

17 November 1973

TETON VILLAGE

Snow mountain fields
seen thru transparent wings
of a fly on the windowpane.

29 Nov. 1973

SWEET BOY, GIMME YR ASS

lemme kiss your face, lick your neck
touch your lips, tongue tickle tongue end
nose to nose, quiet questions
ever slept with a man before?
hand stroking your back slowly down to the cheeks' moist
    hair soft asshole
eyes to eyes blur, a tear strained from seeing—

Come on boy, fingers thru my hair
Pull my beard, kiss my eyelids, tongue my ear, lips light on
    my forehead
—met you in the street you carried my package—
Put your hand down to my legs,
touch if it's there, the prick shaft delicate
hot in your rounded palm, soft thumb on cockhead—

Come on come on kiss me full lipped, wet tongue, eyes open—
animal in the zoo looking out of skull cage—you
smile, I'm here so are you, hand tracing your abdomen
from nipple down rib cage smooth skinn'd past belly veins,
    along muscle to your silk-shiny groin
across the long prick down your right thigh
up the smooth road muscle wall to titty again—
Come on go down on me your throat
swallowing my shaft to the base tongue
cock solid suck—
I'll do the same your stiff prick's soft skin, lick your ass—

Come on Come on, open up, legs apart here this pillow
under your buttock
Come on take it here's vaseline the hard on here's
your old ass lying easy up in the air—here's
a hot prick at yr soft mouthed asshole—just relax and let it in—
Yeah just relax hey Carlos lemme in, I love you, yeah how
     come
you came here anyway except this kiss arms round my neck
                           mouth open your
    two eyes looking up, this hard slow thrust this
        softness this relaxed sweet sigh?

3 January 1974

JAWEH AND ALLAH BATTLE

Jaweh with Atom Bomb
      Allah cuts throat of Infidels
Jaweh's armies beat down neighboring tribes
Will Red Sea waters close & drown th'armies of Allah?

Israel's tribes worshipping the Golden Calf
        Moses broke the Tablets of Law.

Zalmon Schacter Lubovitcher Rebbe what you say
     Stone Commandments broken on the ground
   Sufi Sam whaddya say
     Shall Prophet's companions dance circled
round Synagogue while Jews doven bearded electric?

Both Gods Terrible! Awful Jaweh Allah!
      Both hook-nosed gods, circumcised.
Jaweh Allah which unreal?
              Which stronger Illusion?
                 Which stronger Army?
       Which gives most frightening command?
What God maintain egohood in Eden? Which be Nameless?
          Which enter Abyss of Light?
Worlds of Gods, jealous Warriors, Humans, Animals & Flowers,
     Hungry Ghosts, even Hell Beings all die,
   Snake cock and pig eat each other's tails & perish
All Jews all Moslems'll die All Israelis all Arabs

Cairo's angry millions Jerusalem's multitudes
    suffer Death's dream Armies in battle!
Yea let Tribes wander to tin camps at cold Europe's walls?
Yea let the Million sit in desert shantytowns with tin cups?
I'm a Jew cries Allah! Buddha circumcised!
                Snake sneaking an apple to Eden—
        Alien, Wanderer, Caller of the Great Call!
What Prophet born on this ground
              bound me Eternal to Palestine
    circled by Armies tanks, droning bomber motors,
             radar electric computers?
What Mind directed Stern Gang Irgun Al Fatah
                Black September?
Meyer Lansky? Nixon Shah? Gangster? Premier? King?
              one-eyed General Dayan?
    Golda Meir & Kissinger bound me with Arms?
HITLER AND STALIN SENT ME HERE!
    WEITZMANN & BEN GURION SENT ME HERE!
      NASSER AND SADAT SENT ME HERE!
ARAFAT SENT ME HERE! MESSIAH SENT ME HERE!
           GOD SENT ME HERE!
    Buchenwald sent me here! Vietnam sent me here!
    My-Lai sent me here!
             Lidice sent me here!
My mother sent me here!
        I WAS BORN HERE IN ISRAEL, Arab
    circumcised, my father had a coffee shop in Jerusalem
One day the Soldiers came & told me to walk down road
             my hands up
    walk away leave my house business forever!

The Israelis sent me here!
Solomon's Temple the Pyramids & Sphinx sent me here!
JAWEH AND ALLAH SENT ME HERE!
Abraham will take me to his bosom!
Mohammed will guide me to Paradise!
Christ sent me here to be crucified!
Buddha will wipe us out and destroy the world.
The New York Times and Cairo Editorialist Heykal
sent me here!
Commentary and *Palestine Review* sent me here!
The International Zionist Conspiracy sent me here!
Syrian Politicians sent me here! Heroic Pan-Arab
Nationalists sent me here!
They're sending Armies to my side—
The Americans & Russians are sending bombing planes tanks
Chinese Egyptians Syrians help me battle for my righteous
house my Soul's dirt Spirit's Nation body's
boundaries & Self's territory my
Zionist homeland my Palestine inheritance
The Capitalist Communist & Third World Peoples'
Republics Dictatorships Police States Socialisms
& Democracies
are all sending Deadly Weapons to our aid!
We shall triumph over the Enemy!
Maintain our Separate Identity! Proud
History evermore!
Defend our own bodies here this Holy Land! This hill
Golgotha never forget, never relinquish

inhabit thru Eternity
under Allah Christ Yaweh forever one God
Shema Yisroel Adonoi Eluhenud Adonoi Echad!
La Illaha Illa 'llah Hu!

OY!　AH!　HU!　　　OY!　AH!　HU!
SHALOM!　SHANTIH!　SALAAM!

January 13, 1974

MANIFESTO

Let me say beginning I don't believe in Soul
The heart, famous heart's a bag of shit I wrote 25 years ago
O my immortal soul! youthful poet Shelley cried
O my immortal Ego—little knowing
he didn't believe in God. Neither do I.
Nor all science reason reality and good moral Will—
collections of empty atoms as Kerouac Buddha scribed.

Neither does great love immortal defy pain nightmare Death
        Torture Saigon Police Underground Press Pravda Bill
        of Rights—
And while we're at it, let's denounce Democracy, Fascism,
        Communism and heroes.
Art's not empty if it shows its own emptiness
Poetry useful leaves its own skeleton hanging in air
like Buddha, Shakespeare & Rimbaud.
Serious, dispense with law except Cause & Effect, even the
        latter has exceptions
No cause & effect is not foolproof.
There is Awareness—which confounds the Soul, Heart, God,
        Science Love Governments and Cause & Effects' Night-
        mare.

28 Jan 1974 1 am

SAD DUST GLORIES

To the Dead

You were here on earth, in cities—
                    where now?
Bones in the ground,
              thoughts in my mind.

                    *

Teacher
bring me to heaven
or leave me alone.
Why make me work so hard
when everything's spread around
open, like forest's poison oak
                    turned red
empty sleepingbags hanging from
          a dead branch.

                    *

When I sit
I see dust motes in my eye
Ponderosa needles trembling
              shine green
in blue sky.
Wind sound passes thru
              pine tops, distant
windy waves flutter black
              oak leaves
and leave them still
like my mind
which forgets
why the bluejay across the woods'
                        clearing
squawks, mid afternoon.

                    *

The mood

is sadness, dead friends,
or the boy I slept with last night
came twice silently
and I still lie in the colored
              hammock, half naked
reading poetry
Sunday
in bright sun pine shade.

                    *

Kenji Myazawa

"All is Buddhahood
to who has cried even once
Glory be?"
So I said glory be
        looking down at a pine
                    feather
risen beside a dead leaf
on brown duff
where a fly wavers an inch
            above ground
midsummer.

                    *

Could you be here?
Really be here
        and forget the void?
I am, it's peaceful, empty,
filled with green Ponderosa
    swaying parallel tops
fan like needle circles
glittering haloed
in sun that moves slowly
    lights up my hammock
        heats my face skin
                and knees.

                *

Wind makes sound
     in tree tops
like express trains like city
       machinery
Slow dances high up, huge
     branches wave back &
        forth sensitive
     needlehairs bob their heads
—it's too human, it's not
     human
It's treetops, whatever they think,
It's me, whatever I think,
It's the wind talking.

         ***

The moon followed by Jupiter thru pinetrees,

A mosquito comes round your head buzzing
you know he's going to bite you if he can—

First you look at your thoughts
then you look at the moon
then look at the reflection of the moon in your eyeball
    splatter of light on surface retina
       opening and closing the blotched circle
and the mosquito buzzes, disturbing your senses
    and you remember your itching thumb as mind
             wanders again.

     *

Shobo-an

The Acorn people
    read newspapers
        by kerosene light.

*

By Kitkitdizze Pond in June with Gary Snyder

    Bookkeeping in the moonlight
        —"frogs count
            my checks."

*

    Driving Volkswagen
        with tired feet
    returned from camping
        in Black Buttes
    thru sad dust glories
    turning off Malakoff
        Diggings road
    Blinded by sunlight
        squirrel in
            windshield.

*

September, 1974

EGO CONFESSION

I want to be known as the most brilliant man in America
Introduced to Gyalwa Karmapa heir of the Whispered Trans-
    mission Crazy Wisdom Practice Lineage
as the secret young wise man who visited him and winked
    anonymously decade ago in Gangtok
Prepared the way for Dharma in America without mentioning
    Dharma — scribbled laughter
Who saw Blake and abandoned God
To whom the Messianic Fink sent messages darkest hour
    sleeping on steel sheets "somewhere in the Federal
    Prison system" Weathermen got no Moscow Gold
who went backstage to Cecil Taylor serious chat chord struc-
    ture & Time in nightclub
who fucked a rose-lipped rock star in a tiny bedroom slum
    watched by a statue of Vajrasattva —
and overthrew the CIA with a silent thought —
Old Bohemians many years hence in Viennese beergardens'll
    recall
his many young lovers with astonishing faces and iron breasts
gnostic apparatus and magical observation of rainbow-lit
    spiderwebs
extraordinary cooking, lung stew & Spaghetti a la Vongole
    and recipe for salad dressing 3 parts oil one part vinegar
    much garlic and honey a spoonful
his extraordinary ego, at service of Dharma and completely
    empty
unafraid of its own self's spectre

parroting gossip of gurus and geniuses famous for their reti-
    cence —
Who sang a blues made rock stars weep and moved an old
    black guitarist to laughter in Memphis —
I want to be the spectacle of Poesy triumphant over trickery of
    the world
Omniscient breathing its own breath thru War tear gas spy
    hallucination
whose common sense astonished gaga Gurus and rich
    Artistes —
who called the Justice department & threaten'd to Blow the
    Whistle
Stopt Wars, turned back petrochemical Industries' Captains
    to grieve & groan in bed
Chopped wood, built forest houses & established farms
distributed monies to poor poets & nourished imaginative
    genius of the land
Sat silent in jazz roar writing poetry with an ink pen —
wasn't afraid of God or Death after his 48th year —
let his brains turn to water under Laughing Gas his gold
    molar pulled by futuristic dentists
Seaman knew ocean's surface a year
carpenter late learned bevel and mattock
son, conversed with elder Pound & treated his father gently
— All empty all for show, all for the sake of Poesy
to set surpassing example of sanity as measure for late gener-
    ations
Exemplify Muse Power to the young avert future suicide
accepting his own lie & the gaps between lies with equal good
    humor

Solitary in worlds full of insects & singing birds all solitary
—who had no subject but himself in many disguises
some outside his own body including empty air-filled space
    forests & cities—
Even climbed mountains to create his mountain, with ice ax
    & crampons & ropes, over Glaciers—

October 1974

MUGGING

I .

Tonite I walked out of my red apartment door on East tenth
　　street's dusk —
Walked out of my home ten years, walked out in my honking
　　neighborhood
Tonite at seven walked out past garbage cans chained to con-
　　crete anchors
Walked under black painted fire escapes, giant castiron plate
　　covering a hole in ground
—Crossed the street, traffic lite red, thirteen bus roaring by
　　liquor store,
past corner pharmacy iron grated, past Coca Cola & My-Lai
　　posters fading scraped on brick
Past Chinese Laundry wood door'd, & broken cement stoop
　　steps For Rent hall painted green & purple Puerto Rican
　　style
Along E. 10th's glass splattered pavement, kid blacks & Span-
　　ish oiled hair adolescents' crowded house fronts —
Ah, tonite I walked out on my block NY City under humid
　　summer sky Halloween,
thinking what happened Timothy Leary joining brain police
　　for a season?
thinking what's all this Weathermen, secrecy & selfrighteous-
　　ness beyond reason — F.B.I. plots?
Walked past a taxicab controlling the bottle strewn curb —

past young fellows with their umbrella handles & canes
    leaning against a ravaged Buick
—and as I looked at the crowd of kids on the stoop—a boy
    stepped up, put his arm around my neck
tenderly I thought for a moment, squeezed harder, his um-
    brella handle against my skull,
and his friends took my arm, a young brown companion
    tripped his foot 'gainst my ankle—
as I went down shouting Om Ah Hūm to gangs of lovers on
    the stoop watching
slowly appreciating, why this is a raid, these strangers mean
    strange business
with what—my pockets, bald head, broken-healed-bone leg,
    my softshoes, my heart—
Have they knives? Om Ah Hūm—Have they sharp metal
    wood to shove in eye ear ass? Om Ah Hūm
& slowly reclined on the pavement, struggling to keep my
    woolen bag of poetry address calendar & Leary-lawyer
    notes hung from my shoulder
dragged in my neat orlon shirt over the crossbar of a broken
    metal door
dragged slowly onto the fire-soiled floor an abandoned store,
    laundry candy counter 1929—
now a mess of papers & pillows & plastic car seat covers
    cracked cockroach-corpsed ground—
my wallet back pocket passed over the iron foot step guard
and fell out, stole by God Muggers' lost fingers, Strange—
Couldn't tell—snakeskin wallet actually plastic, 70 dollars
    my bank money for a week,

old broken wallet — and dreary plastic contents — Amex card
    & Manf. Hanover Trust Credit too — business card from
    Mr. Spears British Home Minister Drug Squad — my
    draft card — membership ACLU & Naropa Institute
    Instructor's identification
Om Ah Hūm I continued chanting Om Ah Hūm
Putting my palm on the neck of an 18 year old boy fingering
    my back pocket crying "Where's the money"
"Om Ah Hūm there isn't any"
My card Chief Boo-Hoo Neo American Church New Jersey
    & Lower East Side
Om Ah Hūm — what not forgotten crowded wallet — Mobil
    Credit, Shell? old lovers addresses on cardboard pieces,
    booksellers calling cards —
— "Shut up or we'll murder you" — "Om Ah Hūm take it easy"
Lying on the floor shall I shout more loud? — the metal door
    closed on blackness
one boy felt my broken healed ankle, looking for hundred
    dollar bills behind my stocking weren't even there — a
    third boy untied my Seiko Hong Kong watch rough from
    right wrist leaving a clasp-prick skin tiny bruise
"Shut up and we'll get out of here" — and so they left,
as I rose from the cardboard mattress thinking Om Ah Hūm
    didn't stop em enough,
the tone of voice too loud — my shoulder bag with 10,000
    dollars full of poetry left on the broken floor —

Nov 2, 1974

I I

Went out the door dim eyed, bent down & picked up my
   glasses from step edge I placed them while dragged in
   the store — looked out —

Whole street a bombed-out face, building rows' eyes & teeth
   missing

burned apartments half the long block, gutted cellars, hall-
   ways' charred beams

hanging over trash plaster mounded entrances, couches &
   bedsprings rusty after sunset

Nobody home, but scattered stoopfuls of scared kids frozen
   in black hair

chatted giggling at house doors in black shoes, families
   cooked For Rent some six story houses mid the street's
   wreckage

Nextdoor Bodega, a phone, the police? "I just got mugged"
   I said

to man's face under fluorescent grocery light tin ceiling —

puffy, eyes blank & watery, sickness of beer kidney and
   language tongue

thick lips stunned as my own eyes, poor drunken Uncle
   minding the store!

O hopeless city of idiots empty eyed staring afraid, red beam
   top'd car at street curb arrived —

"Hey maybe my wallet's still on the ground got a flashlight?"

Back into the burnt-doored cave, & the policeman's grey
   flashlight broken no eyebeam —

"My partner all he wants is sit in the car never gets out Hey
   Joe bring your flashlight —"

a tiny throwaway beam, dim as a match in the criminal dark
"No I can't see anything here" . . . "Fill out this form"
Neighborhood street crowd behind a car "We didn't see
     nothing"
Stoop young girls, kids laughing "Listen man last time I
     messed with them see this—"
rolled up his skinny arm shirt, a white knife scar on his brown
     shoulder
"Besides we help you the cops come don't know anybody we
     all get arrested
go to jail I never help no more mind my business everytime"
"Agh!" upstreet think "Gee I don't know anybody here ten
     years lived half block crost Avenue C
and who knows who?"—passing empty apartments, old lady
     with frayed paper bags
sitting in the tin-boarded doorframe of a dead house.

December 10, 1974

WHO RUNS AMERICA?

Oil brown smog over Denver
Oil red dung colored smoke
level to level across the horizon
    blue tainted sky   above
Oil car smog gasoline
       hazing red Denver's day
         December bare trees
            sticking up from housetop streets
Plane lands rumbling, planes rise over
        radar wheels, black smoke
           drifts wobbly from tailfins

Oil millions of cars speeding the cracked plains
Oil from Texas, Bahrein, Venezuela Mexico
Oil that turns General Motors
      revs up Ford
   lights up General Electric, oil that crackles
thru International Business Machine computers,
        charges dynamos for ITT
      sparks Western Electric
          runs thru Amer Telephone & Telegraph wires
Oil that flows thru Exxon New Jersey hoses,
rings in Mobil gas tank cranks, rumbles
          Chrysler engines
shoots thru Texaco pipelines,
     blackens ocean from broken Gulf tankers

spills onto Santa Barbara beaches from
        Standard of California derricks offshore.

3 Dec 1974

Note: The dozen corporations name-dropped herein are top twelve capital Powers whose $133 billion Sales represented a tenth the total Gross National Product one yearly trillion $. Traditionally, an Oil corporation representative fills Post of U.S. Secty. of State and Auto corporation representative fills Secretary of Defense Post. This gossip's source is conversation with Daniel Ellsberg & Gary Snyder Nov. 26, 1974 re: Douglas F. Dowd's *The Twisted Dream, Capitalist Development in the United States Since 1776.* (2nd edition, Cambridge, Winthrop, 1977)　—A.G.

WE RISE ON SUN BEAMS AND FALL IN THE NIGHT

Dawn's orb orange-raw shining over Palisades
bare crowded branches bush up from marshes—
New Jersey with my father riding automobile
highway to Newark Airport—Empire State's
spire, horned buildingtops, Manhattan
rising as in W. C. Williams' eyes between wire trestles—
trucks sixwheeled steady rolling overpass
beside New York—I am here
tiny under sun rising in vast white sky,
staring thru skeleton new buildings,
with pen in hand awake . . .

December 11, 1974

WRITTEN ON HOTEL NAPKIN:
CHICAGO FUTURES

Wind mills churn on Windy City's
    rooftops   Antennae
      collecting electric
above thick-loamed gardens
    on Playboy Tower
Merchandise Mart's compost
          privies
    supply nightsoil for Near North Side's
        back Gardens
Cabbages, celery & cucumbers
    sprout in Mayor Daley's
        frontyard
    rich with human waste —
Bathtub beer like old days
Backyard Mary Jane like
      old days,
Sun reflectors gather heat
    in rockpile collectors
      under apartment walls
Horses graze in Parks &
    streets covered with grass
Mafia Dons shovel earth
      & bury Cauliflower
        leaves
Old gangsters & their sons
    tending grapevines

            mid-March 1975

HOSPITAL WINDOW

At gauzy dusk, thin haze like cigarette smoke
ribbons past Chrysler Building's silver fins
tapering delicately needletopped, Empire State's
taller antenna filmed milky lit amid blocks
black and white apartmenting veil'd sky over Manhattan,
offices new built dark glassed in blueish heaven — The East
50's & 60's covered with castles & watertowers, seven storied
tar-topped house-banks over York Avenue, late may-green
    trees
surrounding Rockefellers' blue domed medical arbor —
Geodesic science at the waters edge — Cars running up
East River Drive, & parked at N.Y. Hospital's oval door
where perfect tulips flower the health of a thousand sick souls
trembling inside hospital rooms. Triboro bridge steel-spiked
raftertops stand stone-piered over mansard
penthouse orange roofs, sunset tinges the river and in a few
Bronx windows, some magnesium vapor brilliances're
spotted five floors above E 59th St under grey painted bridge
trestles. Way downtown along the river, as Monet saw
    Thames
100 years ago, Con Edison smokestacks 14th street,
& Brooklyn Bridge's skeined dim in modern mists —
Pipes sticking up to sky nine smokestacks huge visible —
a little white sharklike helicopter stroboscope blinking
flapping noises descends for some rich invalid under
the Bridge? — "lands on the garbage pier, Department of
    Sanitation"

U.N. Building hangs under an orange crane, & red lights on
vertical avenues below the trees turn green at the nod
of a skull with a mild nerve ache. Dim dharma, I return
to this spectacle after weeks of poisoned lassitude, my thighs
belly chest & arms covered with poxied welts,
head pains fading back of the neck, right eyebrow cheek
mouth paralyzed—from taking the wrong medicine, sweated
too much in the forehead helpless, covered my rage from
gorge to prostate with grinding jaw and tightened anus
not released the weeping scream of horror at robot Mayaguez
World self ton billions metal grief unloaded
Pnom Penh to Nakon Thanom, Santiago & Tehran.
Fresh warm breeze in the window, day's release
from pain, cars float downside the bridge trestle
and uncounted building-wall windows multiplied a mile
deep into ash-delicate sky beguile
my empty mind. A seagull passes alone wings
spread silent over roofs.

May 20, 1975 Mayaguez Crisis

HADDA BE PLAYING ON THE JUKEBOX

Hadda be flashing like the Daily Double
Hadda be playing on TeeVee
Hadda be loudmouthed on the Comedy Hour
Hadda be announced over Loud Speakers
CIA & Mafia are in Cahoots
Hadda be said in old ladies' language
Hadda be said in American Headlines
Kennedy stretched & smiled & got doublecrossed by low life
    goons & Agents
Rich bankers with Criminal Connections
Dope pushers in CIA working with dope pushers from Cuba
working with Big Time syndicate Tampa Florida
Hadda be said with big mouth
Hadda be moaned over Factory foghorns
Hadda be chattered on Car Radio News Broadcast
Hadda be screamed in the kitchen
Hadda be yelled in the basement where uncles were fighting
Hadda be Howled on the streets by Newsboys to bus
    conductors
Hadda be foghorned into N.Y. Harbor
Hadda echo under hard hats
Hadda turn up the Volume in University ballrooms
Hadda be written in library books, footnoted
Hadda be in headlines of the *Times* & *Le Monde*
Hadda be barked over TV
Hadda be heard in side alleys thru bar room doors
Hadda be played on Wire Services
Hadda be bells ringing, Comedians stopt dead in the middle

of a joke in Las Vegas,

Hadda be FBI chief J. E. Hoover & Frank Costello syndicate
mouthpiece meeting in Central Park together weekends
in N.Y. reported posthumously *Time* magazine

Hadda be the Mafia & CIA together

started War on Cuba Bay of Pigs & Poison assassination head-
lines

Hadda be the Dope Cops & the Mafia

sold all that Heroin in America

Hadda be FBI & Organized Crime working together in
Cahoots "against the Commies"

let Lucky Luciano out of Jail take over Sicily Mediterranean
drug trade

Hadda be Corsican goons in Office Strategic Services' Pay
busted 1948 dock strikes in Marseilles, 'sixties port trans-
shipment Indochina heroin,

Hadda be ringing on Multinational Cashregisters

world-wide laundry for organized Criminal money

Hadda be CIA & Mafia & FBI together

bigger than Nixon, bigger than War.

Hadda be a gorged throat full of murder

Hadda be mouth and ass a solid mass of rage

a Red hot head, a scream in the back of the throat

Hadda be in Kissinger's brain

Hadda be in Rockefeller's mouth

Hadda be Central Intelligence The Family "Our Thing" the
Agency Mafia Organized Crime FBI Dope Cops & Multi-
national Corporations

one big set of Criminal gangs working together in Cahoots

Hit Men murderers everywhere outraged, on the make

Secret drunk Brutal Dirty Rich

on top of a Slag heap of prisons, Industrial Cancer, plutonium
    smog, garbaged cities, grandmas' bedsores, Fathers'
    resentments
Hadda be the Rulers wanted Law & Order *they* got rich on
wanted Protection status quo, wanted Junkies wanted Attica
    Wanted Kent State Wanted War in Indochina
Hadda be CIA & the Mafia & the FBI
Multinational Capitalists' Strong arms squads, "Private
    detective Agencies for the very rich"
And their Armies, Navies and Air Force bombing Planes,
Hadda be Capitalism the Vortex of this rage, this
competition man to man, horses' heads in the Capo's bed, turf
    & rumbles, hit men, gang wars across oceans,
bombing Cambodia settled the score when Soviet Pilots
    manned Egyptian fighter planes
Chile's red democracy bumped off with White House pots &
    pans a warning to Mediterranean governments
Secret Police embraced for decades, NKVD & CIA keep
    eachother's secrets, OGPU & DIA never hit their own,
    KGB & FBI one mind — brute force
world-wide, and full of money
Hadda be rich, hadda be powerful, hadda hire technology
    from Harvard
Hadda murder in Indonesia 500,000
Hadda murder in Indochina 2,000,000
Hadda murder in Czechoslovakia
Hadda murder in Chile
Hadda murder in Russia
Hadda murder in America

3 AM May 30, 1975

SICKNESS BLUES

Lord Lord I got the sickness blues, I must've done something
wrong
There ain't no Lord to call on, now my youth is gone.

Sickness blues, don't want to fuck no more
Sickness blues, can't get it up no more
Tears come in my eyes, feel like an old tired whore

I went to see the doctor, he shot me with poison germs
I got out of the hospital, my head was full of worms

All I can think is Death, father's getting old
He can't walk half a block, his feet feel cold

I went down to Santa Fe take vacation there
Indians selling turquoise in dobe huts in Taos Pueblo Square
Got headache in La Fonda, I could get sick anywhere

Must be my bad karma, fuckin these pretty boys
Hungry ghosts chasing me, because I been chasing joys
Lying here in bed alone, playing with my toys

I musta been doing something wrong meat & cigarettes
Bow down before my lord, 100 thousand regrets
All my poems down in hell, that's what pride begets

Sick and angry, lying in my hospital bed
Doctor Doctor bring morphine before I'm totally dead
Sick and angry at the national universe O my aching head

Someday I'm gonna get out of here, go somewhere alone
Yeah I'm going to leave this town with noise of rattling bone
I got the sickness blues, you'll miss me when I'm gone

July 19, 1975

SICKNESS BLUES

Lord lord I got the sickness blues   musta done somep'n wrong   Lord lord I got the sickness blues   I musta done somep'n   wrong   There aint no lord to call on now my youth is gone   Sickness blues, don't wanna fuck no more   Yeah Sickness blues can't get it up no more   Tears come in my eyes   feel like an old tired whore

TRANSCRIBED BY ARTHUR RUSSELL N.Y.C.

COME ALL YE BRAVE BOYS

Come all you young men that proudly display
Your torsos to the Sun on upper Broadway
Come sweet hearties mighty with girls
So lithe and naked to kiss their gold curls
Come beautiful boys with breasts bright gold
Lie down in bed with me ere ye grow old,
Take down your blue jeans, we'll have some raw fun
Lie down on your bellies I'll fuck your soft bun.

Come heroic half naked young studs
That drive automobiles through vaginal blood
Come thin breasted boys and fat muscled kids
With sturdy cocks you deal out green lids
Turn over spread your strong legs like a lass
I'll show you the thrill to be jived up the ass
Come sweet delicate strong minded men
I'll take you thru graveyards & kiss you again

You'll die in your life, wake up in my arms
Sobbing and hugging & showing your charms
Come strong darlings tough children hard boys
Transformed with new tenderness, taught new joys
We'll lie embrac'd in full moonlight till dawn
Whiteness shows sky high over the wet lawn
Lay yr head on my shoulder kiss my lined brow
& belly to belly kiss my neck now

Yeah come on tight assed & strong cocked young fools
& shove up my belly your hard tender tools,
Suck my dick, lick my arm pit and breast
Lie back & sigh in the dawn for a rest,
Come in my arms, groan your sweet will
Come again in my mouth, lie silent & still,
Let me come in your butt, hold my head on your leg,
Let's come together, & tremble & beg.

25 Aug '75 4 AM

CABIN IN THE ROCKIES

I

Against brown grass
　　the hole in the black truck tire
　　　　swings slowly between trees.

Sunlight mixed with dust
　　rises behind a truck
　　　　on the dirt road.

I I

Sitting on a tree stump with half cup of tea,
　　sun down behind mountains—
　　　　Nothing to do.

Not a word! Not a Word!
Flies do all my talking for me—
and the wind says something else.

Fly on my nose,
I'm not the Buddha,
There's no enlightenment here!

Against red bark trunk
   A fly's shadow
lights on the shadow of a pine bough.

An hour after dawn
I haven't thought of Buddha once yet!
—walking back into the retreat house.

I I I

Walking into King Sooper after Two-week Retreat

A thin redfaced pimpled boy
    stands alone minutes
looking down into the ice cream bin.

Sept 16, 1975
Boulder, Colorado

GOSPEL NOBLE TRUTHS

Born in this world you got to suffer —
— everything changes
you got no soul try to be gay
ignorant happy — you get the blues —
you eat jelly-roll —

TRANSCRIBED by ARTHUR RUSSELL N.Y.C.

GOSPEL NOBLE TRUTHS

Born in this world
You got to suffer
Everything changes
You got   no soul

Try to be gay
Ignorant   happy
You get the blues
You eat jellyroll

There is one Way
You take the high road
In your big Wheel
8 steps you fly

Look at the View
Right to horizon
Talk to the sky
Act like you talk

Work like the sun
Shine in your heaven
See what you done
Come down & walk

Sit   you sit down
Breathe when you breathe
Lie down   you lie down
Walk where you walk

Talk when you talk
Cry when you cry
Lie down   you lie down
Die when you die

Look when you look
Hear what you hear
Taste what you taste   here
Smell what you smell

Touch what you touch
Think what you think
Let go Let it go   Slow
Earth Heaven & Hell

Die when you die
Die when you die
Lie down   you lie down
Die when you die

October 17, 1975

LAY DOWN YR MOUNTAIN

LAY DOWN LAY DOWN YR MOUNTAIN

LAY DOWN GOD LAY DOWN

LAY DOWN YR MUSIC LOVE LAY DOWN

LAY DOWN LAY DOWN YR HATRED

LAY YRSELF DOWN LAY DOWN

LAY DOWN YOUR NATION LAY YOUR FOOT ON THE ROCK

LAY DOWN YR WHOLE CRE-A-TION LAY YR

MIND DOWN LAY DOWN LAY DOWN YR EMPIRE

LAY YOUR WHOLE WORLD DOWN, etc.

transcribed by BRIAN MUNEY
NAROPA INSTITUTE
BOULDER, COLO. 7/2/77

ROLLING THUNDER STONES

I

LAY DOWN YR MOUNTAIN

Lay down   Lay down yr mountain   Lay down God
Lay down   Lay down your music   Love lay down

Lay down   Lay down yr hatred   Lay yrself down
Lay down   Lay down your nation   Lay your foot on the rock

Lay down yr whole creation   Lay yr mind down
Lay down   Lay down yr empire   Lay your whole world down

Lay down your soul forever   Lay your vision down
Lay down yr bright body   Down your golden heavy crown

Lay down   Lay down yr magic hey! Alchemist lay it down
                                                    clear
Lay down your practice precisely   Lay down yr wisdom dear

Lay down yr camera   Lay down yr image right
Lay down your image   Lay down light

Lay down   your ignorance   Roll yr wheel once more
Lay down yr suffering   Lay down yr Lion's Roar

October 31, 1975 Midnight addenda 1976

II

**Sunrise Ceremony Verse
improvised with Australian Aborigine Song-sticks
at request of Medicine-man Rolling Thunder Nov. 5, 1975**

When Music was needed Music sounded
When a Ceremony was needed a Teacher appeared
When Students were needed Telephones rang.
When Cars were needed Wheels rolled in
When a Place was needed a Mansion appeared
When a Fire was needed Wood appeared
When an Ocean was needed Waters rippled waves
When Shore was needed Shore met Ocean
When Sun was needed the Sun rose east
When People were needed People arrived
When a circle was needed a Circle was formed.

III

SNOW BLUES

Nobody saves America by sniffing cocaine
Jiggling yr knees blankeyed in the rain
When it snows in yr nose you catch cold in yr brain

Nov. 10, 1975

IV

TO THE SIX NATIONS AT TUSCARORA RESERVATION

We give thanks for this food, deer meat & indian-corn soup
Which is a product of the labor of your people
And the suffering of other forms of life
And which we promise to transform into friendly song and
dancing
To all the ten directions of the Earth.

(After Snyder/Whalen Adaptation of Zen thanks-offering for food)

Nov 18, 1975

V

Snow falls
souls freeze
Speed kills
heart's ease
Alcohol
fools wills
O slaves
Who craves
junk raves
Downer's
angers
eyes blur—
I sing
Rolling
Thunder
Ho ho!
Macho
frenzy
in thee
's a drag
dead bag.

Smoke grass
Yaas Yaas
Shake ass
mind's wealth
joint's health
Ready?
Medi-
tations
patience
eyes keen
serene
as graves
saves! saves
nations.

Dec. 4, 1975

TWO DREAMS

A

As I passed thru Moscow's grass lots I heard
a voice, a small green dwarf, leaf-clothed &
thin corn-stalk arms, head capped with green
husk & tassel, walking toward me talking:
"You see these other tassel heads stalking
thru long green grass spears half buried
in empty lots where building-ghosts stand
razed by police state but bursting from ground
Springtime as now seeds grown natural
So I full grown sprite of Friendship salute
you who seek love in Roman Moscow circuses—
Be cheerful our enemy's enemy is Death
and since Death is We, since all die, all
is not lost but to Death, & what lives eccentric
as yourself & Me, ancient friends, lives
humorous and democratic as your leaves of grass
which die also prophesied but live as you and I.
Bee cheerful, good Sir. Cockhead green am I
an entertainer triumphant in the tiny cliffs
between buildings, in old grasslots of Paterson
where the wrecker's ball creates a tiny farm
for worms, and bottles glint in new turned earth—
and weeds and we sprout renewing Nature's
humor where the architectural police are on the nod.
The sun will rise and I'll accompany your eye
that walks thru Moscow looking for human love."

B

SLUDGE

Dantean, the cliffside whereon I walked
With volumes of Milton & the Tuscan Bard enarmed:
Highway prospecting th'ocean Sludged transparent
lipped to asphalt built by Man under sky.
Far down below the factory I espied, and plunged
full clothed into the Acid Tide, heroic precipitous
Stupidly swam the noxious surface to my goal—
An Oil platform at land's end, where Fellows watched
my bold approach to the Satanic World Trade Center.

Father dying tumored, Industry smog
o'erspreads dawn sky, gold beams descend
on Paterson thru subtle tar fumes, viewless
to wakened eye, transfused into family meat.
Capitalism's reckless industry cancers New Jersey.

March 6, 1976

DON'T GROW OLD

I

Old Poet, Poetry's final subject glimmers months ahead
Tender mornings, Paterson roofs snowcovered
Vast
Sky over City Hall tower, Eastside Park's grass terraces &
    tennis courts beside Passaic River
Parts of ourselves gone, sister Rose's apartments, brown
    corridor'd high schools—
Too tired to go out for a walk, too tired to end the War
Too tired to save body
too tired to be heroic
The real close at hand as the stomach
liver pancreas rib
Coughing up gastric saliva
Marriages vanished in a cough
Hard to get up from the easy chair
Hands white   feet speckled   a blue toe   stomach big breasts
    hanging thin
hair white on the chest
too tired to take off shoes and black sox

Jan 12, 1976

II

He'll see no more Times Square
honkytonk movie marquees, bus stations at midnight
Nor the orange sun ball
rising thru treetops east toward New York's skyline
His velvet armchair facing the window will be empty
He won't see the moon over house roofs
or sky over Paterson's streets.

Feb 26, 1976

III

Wasted arms, feeble knees
    80 years old, hair thin and white
        cheek bonier than I'd remembered —
head bowed on his neck, eyes opened
    now and then, he listened —
    I read my father Wordsworth's *Intimations of Immortality*
"*. . . trailing clouds of glory do we come
    from God, who is our home . . .*"
        "That's beautiful," he said, "but it's not true."

"When I was a boy, we had a house
    on Boyd Street, Newark — the backyard
        was a big empty lot full of bushes and tall grass,
    I always wondered what was behind those trees,
When I grew older, I walked around the block,
    and found out what was back there —
        it was a glue factory."

May 18, 1976

IV

Will that happen to me?
Of course, it'll happen to thee.

Will my arms whither away?
Yes yr arm hair will turn grey.

Will my knees grow weak & collapse?
Your knees will need crutches perhaps.

Will my chest get thin?
Your breasts will be hanging skin.

Where will go—my teeth?
You'll keep the ones beneath.

What'll happen to my bones?
They'll get mixed up with stones.

June 1976

V

FATHER DEATH BLUES

Hey Father Death, I'm flying home
Hey poor man, you're all alone
Hey old daddy, I know where I'm going

Father Death, Don't cry any more
Mama's there, underneath the floor
Brother Death, please mind the store

Old Aunty Death   Don't hide your bones
Old Uncle Death   I hear your groans
O Sister Death   how sweet your moans

O Children Deaths go breathe your breaths
Sobbing breasts'll ease your Deaths
Pain is gone, tears take the rest

Genius Death   your art is done
Lover Death your body's gone
Father Death   I'm coming home

Guru Death your words are true
Teacher Death I do thank you
For inspiring me to sing this Blues

Buddha Death, I wake with you
Dharma Death, your mind is true
Sangha Death, we'll work it through

Suffering is what was born
Ignorance made me forlorn
Tearful truths I cannot scorn

Father Breath once more farewell
Birth you gave was no thing ill
My heart is still, as time will tell.

July 8, 1976 (over Lake Michigan)

FATHER DEATH BLUES

Hey   Father   Death   I'm   fly-ing   home

Hey   old   man   you're   all   a-lone   Hey   old

Daddy   I   know   where   I'm   going

TRANSCRIBED by ARTHUR RUSSELL
N.Y.C.

VI

Near the Scrap Yard my Father'll be Buried
Near Newark Airport my father'll be
Under a Winston Cigarette sign buried
On Exit 14 Turnpike NJ South
Through the tollgate Service Road 1 my father buried
Past Merchants Refrigerating concrete on the cattailed marshes
past the Budweiser Anheuser-Busch brick brewery
in B'Nai Israel Cemetery behind a green painted iron fence
where there used to be a paint factory and farms
where Pennick makes chemicals now
under the Penn Central power Station
transformers & wires, at the borderline
between Elizabeth and Newark, next to Aunt Rose
Gaidemack, near Uncle Harry Meltzer
one grave over from Abe's wife Anna my father'll be buried.

9 July 1976

VII

What's to be done about Death?
Nothing, nothing
Stop going to school No. 6 in 1937?
Freeze time tonight, with a headache, at quarter to 2 A.M.?
Not go to Father's funeral tomorrow morn?
Not go back to Naropa   teach Buddhist poetics summer?
Not be buried in the cemetery near Newark Airport some day?

July 11, 1976

LAND O' LAKES, WISC.

Buddha died and
left behind a
big emptiness.

October 1976

"DRIVE ALL BLAMES INTO ONE"

It's everybody's fault but me.
I didn't do it. I didn't start the universe.
I didn't steal Dr. Mahler's tiles from his garage roof for my
    chicken coop
where I had six baby chicks I paid for so I could attract
my grammar school boyfriends to play with me in my
    backyard
They stole the tiles I'm going across the street to the candystore
and tell the old uncle behind the glass counter I'm mad at my
    boyfriends
for stealing that slate I took all the blame—
Last night I dreamt they blamed me again on the streetcorner
They got me bent over with my pants down and spanked my
    behind I was ashamed
I was red faced my self was naked I got hot I had a hard on.

October 25, 1976

HAUNTING POE'S BALTIMORE

I

POE IN DUST

Baltimore bones groan maliciously under sidewalk
Poe hides his hideous skeleton under church yard
Equinoctial worms peep thru his mummy ear
The slug rides his skull, black hair twisted in roots of
    threadbare grass
Blind mole at heart, caterpillars shudder in his ribcage,
Intestines wound with garter snakes
midst dry dust, snake eye & gut sifting thru his pelvis
Slimed moss green on his phosphor'd toenails, sole toeing
    black tombstone —
O prophet Poe well writ! your catacomb cranium chambered
eyeless, secret hid to moonlight ev'n under corpse-rich ground
where tread priest, passerby, and poet
staring white-eyed thru barred spiked gates
at viaducts heavy-bound and manacled upon the city's heart.

Jan 10, 1977

II

HEARING "LENORE" READ ALOUD
AT 203 AMITY STREET

The light still gleams reflected from the brazen fire-tongs
The spinet is now silent to the ears of silent throngs
For the Spirit of the Poet, who sang well of brides and ghouls
Still remains to haunt what children will obey his vision's
                                                        rules.

They who weep and burn in houses scattered thick on Jersey's
                                                        shore
Their eyes have seen his ghostly image, though the Prophet
                                                walks no more
Raven bright & cat of Night; and his wines of Death still run
In their veins who haunt his brains, hidden from the
                                                human sun.

Reading words aloud from books, till a century has passed
In his house his heirs carouse, till his woes are theirs at last:
So I saw a pale youth trembling, speaking rhymes Poe spoke
                                                before,
Till Poe's light rose on the living, and His fire gleamed
                                                on the floor —

The sitting room lost its cold gloom, I saw these generations
burn
With the Beauty he abandoned; in new bodies they return:
To inspire future children 'spite his *Raven*'s "Nevermore"
I have writ this antient riddle in Poe's house in Baltimore.

January 16, 1977

CONTEST OF BARDS

I

THE ARGUMENT: Old bard lived in solitary stone house at ocean edge three decades retired from the world, Young poet arrives naked interrupting his studies & announces his own prophetic dreams to replace the old Bard's boring verities. Young poet had dreamed old poet's scene & its hidden secret, an Eternal Rune cut in stone at the hearth-front hidden under porphyry bard-throne. Young bard tries to seduce old Boner with his energy & insight, & makes him crawl down on the floor to read the secret riddle Rhyme.

And the youth free stripling bounding along the Hills of Color
And the old man bearded, wrinkled, browed in his black cave
Meet in the broken house of stone, walls engraven with
    Prophet Hands,
& contend for the Mysteries, vanity against vanity, deciphering
Eternal runes of Love, & Silence, & the Monster of Self
Covered with Blood & Lilies, covered with bones and hair
    and skin:
They glory in Night & Starvation the Fat Bright Cherub of
    Resurrection,
Bliss & God: Terrible Mental Cherub of Chemistry Imagina-
    tion & Vanity
Bard after Bard orating and perishing, casting behind his
    image on men's brains
thru sounds symboled on the mind's stone walls reverberat-

ing Syllables Visionary
Perfect formed to 'dure Millennia, but Phantom is such Rock,
Phantom as the Cellular Believer in's own tangible re-creation.

"I hear the Bard's stone words Build my Immortal Archi-
    tecture:
This body stone hands and genitals   this Heart stone Ten-
    derness
and Delight   This head Stone language to Rafter the Stone
    Bed of Love.
Come lay down on this rock pillow, kid, lay down your tender
    breast,
Pale face, red hair, soft belly   hairy tender foot and Loins
Under the hard immortal blanket, mattress of Rock sheeted
    with Vocables!
In twenty years I'll vanish from this shore & Solitary Eternal
    Cave—
Here I studied & Deciphered the Granite Alphabet surrendered
from Graves from Sands that swirled at the door, from star-fish
spotted boulders in seas' low tide when full-moon-gleam
Pulls bones of Leviathan & tiny bass-fins tide-pool'd
many in ancient nights." So one spoke, ocean serpents curl'd
    around
his whitened beard, eyes wide in horror he be left by the
    Dark Shore,
to burn his memories in the rocky hearth & keep his cold loins
    warm
in winter-rain days or in snowy night's vastness filled
with stars and planets, spring summer & autumn mortality.
Sly, craven, conquering he spoke, his words like rainbows,

or firelight, or shadows, moving humorous thru his beard,
falling in the air, clothing his body in hypocritic webs of truth,
to hide his shame, his empty nakedness. He meditated
remembering deeper Buddhic prophecies, abhoring his own
    runes solid
immovable but by time and storm inexorable, half visible on
    his walls.

The youth the color of the hills laughed delighted at his Vanity
and cried, "Under the hearth stone's a rune, old Bard of
    Familiarity,
your eyes forgot, or tempest-addled brain, so busy boiling
    meat
and tending to your threadbare cares and household hermitage
& fishing day by day for thirty years for thoughts! Behold!"
He naked bent and moved the porphyry-smooth red fire-seat
    aside:
"Read what's writ on earth here before you Ignorant Prophet,
Learn in your age what True Magicians spelled for all
    Futurity,
Cut in the vanity of rock before your feeble hand grasped
    iron Pen
Or feather fancy tickled your gross ear: There have been
    sages here
before you, and I am after to outlive your gloomy miserous
hospitality. I loved you Ungrateful Unimaginative Bard
And Came over hills thru small cities to companion your
    steadfast study.
I dreamed of your eyes and beard and rocks and oceans, I
    dreamed

this room these pitted moss green walls & runes you scraped
deciphered and memorized, pillars worn by tide and smoke
of your lamp   You Grow near blind reading mind on your
    own house walls,
I dreamt you sitting on your fire-seat reading the vaporous
    language of flame tongues
nescient to the airy rune cut in the Bedrock under yr very
    Shamanic Throne
You stare at the ceiling half asleep, or sit on your pillow with
    heavy eyelid
murmuring old bards Truths to your brain, repetitive
imagining me, or some other red-buttocked stripling savior
    come
to yr stone bed naked to renew your old body's intelligence
and help you read again when blind now what you already
    memorized
and forgot, peering like a boor illiterate in Shadows 30
    years—
Yes I have come but not for your feeble purpose, come of my
    own dreamed will
To show you what dream you forgot dreamt, Immortal Text
neglected under your groaning seat as you sat self-inspired
    by your mortal fire.
O Self Absorbed vulgar hungry Demon, leave your body &
    mine
Take eyes off your own veined hands and worm thoughts,
    lower
Your watery selfish infatuate eyes from my breast to my feet
& read me aloud in Bardic Voice, that Voice of Rock you
    boast so well so many decades,

Yea Face inland to the fields and railroads skyscrapers &
   Viaducts,
Youths maddened by Afric jukeboxes & maidens simpering
   at Picture shows
Read thru smokey air to a hopeless hundred millions fools!
Read what young mind's Pearl Majesty made round oracular
   Beauteous
More unworldly than your own self-haunted snaily skull &
   stony household shell."
Pointing downward, his arm stiff in disdain dismissing lesser
   Beauty,
Like radiant lively Adolescence rejecting joy or sorrow,
   shrewd
with bright glance Innocent, albescent limbs ruddy and
   smooth in Sea-Wrack Firelight
Proud with centuries of learning in New-woke brain and
   boyish limbs, so stood the young messenger.

Startled, the wool-wrapped bard looked up at eyes mocking
   shining into his own:
Looked down at the boy's neck unwrinkled white unlike his
   own: the breast
thin muscled unawakened silken flesh: the belly with a corse
   of tawny hair
rosed round the pricked virgin-budding genitals, shining in
   hearth light,
thighs ready and careless like a strong Child's, playful
   walking & dancing tho awkward,
Thick calves with new hair light to the foot long as a man's.

Humbled, bewilderment Touching his tongue,   heart beat-
ing his ribs rewakened

The bard mused on this mortal beauty, remembering dead
bodies he'd embraced in rough and silken beds

Years, years, and years of loves ago—his breast grew light,
eyes lost

in dream—Then in his forehead Time gapped all youthful-
imaged bodies there

Devouring their Shadows, as the sea surged out the rocky
door,

The stars inclined thru cold air, moved so slow blue shining
past

he saw them barely touch the ocean wave and rise and blink
and glimmer silently engulfed—

Then to the Prophesied Task his inner eyes returned to their
dim outward orbs:

Saw the gloom in his own stony shell: stone letters wavering
on chill walls,

Iron Pots carbon black on shelves, old seaweed clothes in a
stone closet, folded green

for Holiday Solitude at Vernal Equinox and full Moon face—
brass fire tongs

from old Paumanok City bought with gold gleaming strong
at the hearth's light—

The hearth seat was moved, the porphyry throne worn
smooth by the sea's muscles

His eyes fell down to the messenger's foot, toes spread firm on
the runed lintel:

THE RUNE

Where the years have gone,   where the clouds have flown
                              Where the rainbow shone
We vanish,   and we make no moan

Where the sun will blind   the delighting mind
                            in a diamond wind
We appear,   our beauty refined.

Icy intellect,   fir'y Beauty wreck
                        but Love's castled speck
of Moonbeam,   nor is Truth correct.

Wise bodies leave here   with the mind's false cheer,
                          Eternity near
as Beauty,   where we disappear.

When sufferings come,   when all tongues lie dumb
                        when Bliss is all numb
with knowledge,   a bony white sum,

We die neither blest   nor with curse confessed
                        wanting Earth's worst Best:
But return,   where all Beauties rest.

Jan 17-22, 1977

The Rune

C   F

Where the years have gone, where the clouds have flown
D   G

Where the rainbow shone we vanish, and we make no moan
C   F   D

Where the sun will blind the delighting mind we diamond wind
G

We appear, our beauty refined ...
C   F

When sufferings come, When all tongues lie dumb When
D   G

Bliss is all numb with knowledge, a bony white sum,
C   F

We die neither blest nor with curse confessed Wanting
D   G   D G

Earth's worst best: But return, where all beauties rest.

FROM CONTEST OF BARDS   FIRST NOTATION ALLEN GINSBERG
May 1977 KESEY'S House → S.F.
Oregon

II

THE ARGUMENT: The Rune having been discovered by the Boy to the Man, the messenger commands the Hermit Sage to go out into the world with him, seek the ancient unearthly Beauty the riddle indicated. The old man gets mad, he says he's near death, has lost Desire. The boy reads his mind and lays down with the sage to make love. At dawn he gets up says he's disgusted with the body, condemns the sage to Chastity, demands the hermit leave his cell forever, and promises to lead him to the land of Poetry in the Sky. Exasperated, the old bard reveals the secret of the mysterious riddle.

And the old man silver bearded gold bald kneeling at his
     black cave's ruddy fireplace
Read the airy verses, humming them to himself, hands to the
     cold floor to support his aching spine
watery eyed, one palsied cheek the muscles of the eyelid weak
dripped with empty tears, unsorrowful soul'd, conning &
     eyeing the bright rhymes' No Truth
Unfrowning, pondering old thought arisen on a breath from
     Meditation's hour—
Inspirations drawing populous-hued tides of living plasm
     thru seaweed pipes
from breast to brain, phantasms of interior ocean freshening
     the surface of the eyeball,
old breath familiar exhaling into starry space that held shore
     & heaven

where sat his tiny stone house, lost in black winds lapped by
  black waters fishy eyed
oft phosphorescent when jellied monster sprites floated to the
  golden sand,
wet bubbles of vehemence mouth'd by a ripple, tiny translucent
  spirits
dried in the eyebeams of the frowning Face o' the moon, with
  the tip of a planet
beaming twinkled deeper in Blackness washed by deep waves
  in the ear.

Dead bearded wise on his knees the old bard stared thru his
  beating universe
At dead stanza'd riddles chiseled with thought & filled with
  wise gold
at the bright colored foot of the boy, reddened by light of
  driftwood afire.
"What is your mind?" yelled the youth, his proud contention
  shaped on red little lips
beardless, ready to argue & instruct for he had dreamed well
  clear accurate
Each stony word, each flame of the hearth fire, each tear in
  the eyelid of the elder Sage,
each silver lock of hair, each worried frown wrinkling that
  skull, each conscious smile
that crept along the thick lipped prophet's lips involuntary,
  who knelt still
at the young teacher's knees — "What Beauty's stopped your
  Poetry! old speaker-forth

of Naked Thoughts?" the ruddy legged messenger laughed
    down, skillful-tongued, black eye beaming merry—
"Will you obey my will and follow me through a riot of cities,
    to delicate-porched countryhouses
& rich polished-marble mansions, where we'll sport with
    Princes & Millionaires
and make fun of the world's kings and Presidents Pomps &
    Limousines all present in their Unbeauty?
Come leave your stupid business of seashells & seawrack,
    gathering wrinkles of the sea?
Come with your pearls and banks of Ambergris hidden under
    yr bed & in yr stone closets?
Come wrapped with seaweed round your belly & Neptunic
    laurel moist on yr skull's half century?
Carry yr vowelic conch & give blast midnights in Midcity
    canyons Wall Street to Washington,
Granite Pillars echoing ocean mouthed pearly syllables
    along Chicago's Lakeshore
& reverberating in Pittsburgh's National Banks—Dance
    with the golden Trident of Fame in Hollywood
Lift the Inspired Lyre to Strike the Ears of hotels in Los
    Angeles?"

The old man changed his thought, and stared in the boy's eye,
    interrupting his beauty—
His voice grown wrathful & ruinous, he lifted himself up on
    his haunches & glared
at the childish youth's face till it paled, brow furrowed in self
    consideration

small mouth open breathing doubtful thoughts, and tiny
   sighs uttered to match his listening.

"Innocent!" the squinting bearded palsied resentful Shaman
   yelled,

"Come over sunshine colored hills naked thru suburbs
   boasting

Your beauty intelligence and sexual joy O Delicate Skulled
   Youth,

You bring news of old prophecy! You wake my wrathful
   Desires!

old lust for mental power and vain body'd joy! Blind craving
   for Bliss

of Breast and Loins! Shadow Conquest! Uncompassionate
   Angel!

Know th' emptiness your own Soul? Think you're a king in
   oceans of Thought?

Neptune himself with his Crown of drown'd gold over a
   beardless face

pale ivory with vanity! Re-waken ignorant desires no mortal
   boy can satisfy?

I go to a death you never dreamed, in iron oceans! homeless
   skull

washed underwave with octopus and seahorse, flicked by soft
   wings of pink fish my eyelids!

Teeth a silver wormhouse on the sandy bottom, polypus &
   green-suckered squid in my ribs, wavy

snake-tailed insensible kelp and water-cactus footed in watery
   loins! clams breathe

their cold valved zephyrs where my heart ached on translucent

shelves! Typhoons carry my voice away!
There is no God or Beauty suffering on earth nor starred in
nebulous blue heaven
but only Dream that floats vast as an Ocean under the moon —
The moon, the cold full moon, boy, fills the window — look at
the sea
waving with lunar glitter like your eye — out there's the moon
Mirror to give back cold pure cheer light on us, fade these
Plutonian Images.
There's a clear light without soul or vanity shining thru the
stone window
shafting square on that rune uncovered at the hearth — the
fire's down but we can read it still —
Hermetic years've passed me by here, Cooled my anger like
this moonlight cools the eye
— my loves & all desires burnt away, like this hearth's wood to
ash."

"Behind the ashes of your face your mind wanders strongly —
what your mind was
I knew as a young boy of books and dreams" the messenger
replied calm voiced
speaking carefully, piping his thoughts intellectual clear in
the old bard's ear —
He settled down on the tiger, deer & sheep-skin covered
floor, where the old man lay
with bearded head uplifted on the gold haired neck of a Lion
amber eyed
Staring silent at the moon, huge pelt outstretched four-
legged with yellow claws

and hard tail laid out on white lamb fleece toward the new
discovered hearth-Rune.

Shivering in moonlight musing at the fire, the messenger put
his nakedness against the white robed Elder's

Giant form, slow-breathed resting back on the soft floor,
silent eyes awake—

"I know your present mind, old heart, I'll satisfy that as you
wish

Unspoken, I know your work & nature beyond the wildest
daydream

Y'ever had naked in hot sunshine summer noon ecstatic far
from mankind

or downy-bearded in your animal bed embraced with glad
phantom heroes

in midnight reverie down below Orion's belt, right hand
clasped in the heat of Creaturehood,

I saw your hard revelry with bodiless immortal companions,"
the messenger cajoled,

laying his mournful sweet visage on the silenced Sage's
shoulder, drawing his right arm down his nippled thin-
ribbed chest.

He shook & trembled chill, for the low moon paled over
green ocean waves

and cold bright sun-fire passed upward whitening the long
horizon—

The cloud-glory'd orange Orb arc'd living in blue still space,
then lifting its bulk aflame

circled slowly over the breathing earth, while tiny oil tankers
moved thru dawn

floating across the widespread ocean's far edge silently going
    from world to world.

The boy took wrinkled years on his flesh, the snow whiskered
    bard trembled and touched
his breast, embracing, adoring from nipple to pink kneecap
and kissing behind him and before, using his form as a girl's.
The youth of colored hills closed his eyes in virgin pleasure,
    uttered small moans
of merciful-limbed ecstasy in his throat, ah tremorous day-
    dream pleasure,
body tingling delicate, made tender, open'd flower-soft, skull
    top to sole skin touched.
The messenger, young and cold as the sun, sad face turned up
    to his earth-worn host
shuddered then as morning warmed the chill world, shuddered
    more than with world's chill
drawing his old Companion closer face to face embraced,
    silent thoughted, calm and still.
The boy looked in his elder's eyes, which gazed in his while
    bare branches on the hillside stood trembling in sky
blue dawn light. Honey bees woke under heaven inland and
    sought the lilac, Honeysuckle, rose,
pale dew dript from day-lily leaf to leaf, green lamps went out
    in windows on Minneapolis avenues,
Lovers rose to work in subways, buses ground down empty
    streets in early light, the country
robin lit from the maple leaf whistling, cat scratched the farm-
    house door
bulls groaned in barns, the aluminum pail clanked on cement

by wooden stools in steaming flop

& stainless-steel mouths sucked milk from millions of cows into shining vats,

Black nannygoats whinnied nubian complaints to the stinking spotted dog

whose clump'd hair hung from his belly tangled with thistle, Church organs sang,

Radios Chattered the nasal weather from barn to barn, the last snow patch slipped from the tarpaper roof of the tractor lean-to,

Ice melted in the willow bog, stars vanished from the sky over gravestones stained with water melt,

The White House shined near pillared Courts on electric-lit avenues wide roaring with cars.

The messenger remembered his dream vision, the Rune discovered by the bright fire,

the Hermit's startled wrath, magnificent and vainly noised all night,

his softness now, his careful fear, the wrinkle that remained around his eye

still watery with emotionless tears tho he held love in his arms, a silent thinking boy.

The naked messenger returned his thought. "I came for Love, old bard, tho you mistook

my youth for Innocence; I came for love, Old Prophet, and I brought you Prophecy,

Though you knew all; I came from Beauty, I came to Beauty, and I brought more beauty.

I knew the Beauty here; not your ass on your stone seat but

under your prophetic throne,

older Beauty than your own, that laughs at wrinkled or smooth loins:

thus I have proved pure Beauty to your empty heart—and now you sigh.

It is that Beauty that I love in you, & not your intestinal self—

A Babe I saw more horror than your smokey ocean holds, your empty heaven,

& your tattered Earth. Follow the Prophecy I showed on your floor

Follow the Ancient Command, chase diamonds in the wind, chase years, chase clouds

chase this rainbow I brought you, chase Beauty again—

chase wrinkled lust away or chase a moonbeam, chase the rising Sun and then Chase setting sun

chase off your Mind thru ocean, chase mind Under the World,

Chase your body down to the grave & rejoice, Chase Chastity at last!

Chaste virgin suffering for you now old bony lecherous Poet."

The boy raged on, with tongue caught fire from the dawn sun lifted now over the heavy

skulled rafters of the hermitage long-haired with sea moss barnacled at foot,

stone girders snailed and starfish stinking, sea sperm rotten in kelp masses

at the porch stone. "Your door's the musty stone door of a tomb, old man,

corpses of corrupted loves're buried under the smooth stone bed we lie on,

pitted with yr fearful tears! What animal skins you vulgarize
    your bed with,
boorish stained with creepy-handed dream stuff jacked out of
    your Impotent loins in Pain—
This toothless lion, stuffed head, ear bit off by sea moths, this
    your love?
Deerskin stol'n from a Dead Buddha, snatched from wander-
    ings in your boring Buddhafields?
A gutless Lamb for a pillow I hear you baah & bleat your
    Terrified Love—
Naked I have you now, bared, wrinkled, heaving heavy
    breaths on me
you brought to your bed, and covered with hides of deskele-
    toned sheep."

Wondering between shame and Longing the old Bard lay thick
    bellied open eyed
Bewilderment at heart, chill-loined, urgent to press that
    Cherry raving angel mouth a soft kiss,
tie down the juvenile prophet on the stone bed back upturned
    to slap his shamed white cheeks
in furious sexual punishment, pubescent weakling pale with
    anger,
rouse his virgin blood to blush thin buttocks ruddy tingling,
    humiliated
cock hard pink with desire, heart tamed submissive, soft
    lipped, tearful.
The kid-like messenger laughed in the bed Despairing and
    looked the old man in the eye:

"Now slap my face, I want to Feel! Hard with all your Love's
  strength coward Bard!

Show your Power!" Bold mute the Bard hit once, and then hit
  hard —

Cold faced, the Boy complained, "Now hit again, I want to feel
  an honest hand!" The old man struck

his naked cheek with a rough palm, thrice shocked by harsh
  joy, pain enough!

"Now!" said the Changeling boy, "We prove the last verse of
  this Prophecy —

Yes the Prophecy old & Confounded Fool, that rune on your
  floor you never beheld before

I forced your gaze to my foot, the prophecy some Elder
  Mysterious Forebear Bard Magician left us —

that prophecy I dreamed & made real before your eyes,
  renewing your Beauty

thru suffering dumb knowledge, yourself roused at my
  Beauteous Command —

All but the Last verse I understand, thick rhymed with senses
  and nonsenses of worst Beauty

no man or boy can interpret in this stupid dank closed cell

Under this Skull that hides the Sun, behind walls covered
  with yr chill laborious decipherings,

your 30 years moony babbling fishy solitude — one verse
  remains undeciphered,

Magical worthy our mutual war thru Society & Nations,
  Bards at large on the planet

seeking to answer the Text! old man of Love I give you my
  virgin mind —

You read my youthful Beauty, tender lip and merry eye or
    Changeling glance

and love you think this silken muscular body, red hair even-
    parted curling round my skull—

Sir I do love you, but hate this earth and myself in it and the
    ignorance

creeping in this house! Sir I do love your beard which you
    know is Beautiful to me,

as beardless my tender-muscled abdomen to you: But my
    Beauty you love most

is that of the aethereal Changeling of Poesy, the same I love
    in you

which Frightens you; then know yourself slave of Immor-
    tality, Master of Unearthly Beauty

nothing less, not God nor Empty Gurus of Thibet not Medita-
    tion's quiet starlit hour

nor aching prostration to the Dharma King nor realms of
    human poetry

washed at your doorstep everymorn by the sea, stamp'd with
    gold sand dollars

licked by scummy wavelets, nor all the old beloved ghost
    boys dead

made famous by your Immortality. Here's rotten Fish,
    Leviathan honor stinks your shore!

and makes this hermit house no more habitable! Leave your
    wordy life behind!

Chase the Last Beauty with me till we find the author, even if
    we enter Death Trance with 'im,

rise & gather your Sea gold, all your grassy Emeralds & cham-
    pagne Amber hidden safe

Under the rune stone at the Hearth Yes Sir your Sparkling
    diamond treasury
I dreamed it well! Clear Sapphires blue as ice you see in sky!
    And hoarded rubies
red & multitudinous enough to make Each maiden and each
    boy on earth blush red with genius joy!
Naked! Naked! rise with me take all your Secrets in the air,
    the Sun's at height, the morning's op'd blue sky,
Grandfather Clocks bong noon in oriental Carpet living-
    rooms in the Capital!
Close the stone door behind you, close this tomb lest gulls
    that swim the sea air
pluck the blind eyes of this lion out of its straw-brained head!
    Come out horrid Corpse!
But memorize the rune before we go, it'll encompass our lov'd
    wanderings!
As Dante had his Virgil & as Blake his own Miltonic Fiend,
    I your Cherub & Punk Idol
'll be Companion of th' Aethereal Ways till we discover of the
    Secret Eidolon
What Beauteous Paradise is spelled, & what the Speller of
    the Stanza was
Who chiseled his unearthly riddle on this floor before I was
    born."

The old bard trembled pale, at last his heart grew cold, com-
    posed to hear the fair youth raving
thru Hells and Heavens, paradise on his red lips, tricking,
    ravening Commanding,

hissing words half-cursed half prayers! Rending the breathing
blue-green globe apart

in Vanity for what is not, aethereal Death and Life, while
Love and sorrow ache

in the breast of the living moment under living skin, breath
thrilled with sigh,

great Death & Life together One & love but a soul Aware,

For mind in heart is one with the body, Truth is the Depth of
that,

and Poetry the Groan of Body lost in the Grave, for Thought
is the love of Earth.

"I knew this Rune once long ago, cold Demon inspired kid,
bright boy —

thank you for discovering it me again, 'twas meant for you to
read in Dreams

and find at your own bare foot one day. I hardly visioned to
be here when you came

naked maddened with delight into my room, demanding I
respect your lips & loins.

Listen now, my turn to tell the story of a day when I was young
as you,

Was in this room, for I was here lone witness to the Stranger,
Alien, Wanderer,

Caller of the Great Call, Serpent minded Messenger that
came like yourself

Naked from Beauty to Beauty. He came in the door as you
did, but no one was home

to greet him, make fire to shine on runes or warm him in beds
of Power, Wrath and

Meditation, Service or Tenderness. Nor was Sea gold gathered
   No nor any rhymed
or unrhymed Rune, not in this house on America's Eastern
   Shore.
Some house was here before, but broken down a Century
   Past, & Uninhabitable.
I gathered icy diamonds in the salt sea, plucked the blue eye
   of the whale for wisdom,
Green emeralds I found in the growing grass and on tree
   boughs in their Springtime buds,
For thirty years enriched with witty penury I gathered
   Amber from the generous laurel
and Rubies rolled out of my heart. I threw away the Pearl,
   back to the sea
To keep God out of trouble under his blue net blanket, and
   be done
with clammy envy and his watery blisses and grasping
   waves.
I brought the shining fire tongs here from Bardic Manahatta,
   & the Red Porphyry Chair of Poetry
from the Ind. I set it beside the hearth and built a fire out of
   seawracked thrones of wooden kings
I found on the illuminated shore, and lay down on my belly
   in my healthy youth
and Carved your Beauteous riddle on this bedrock basalt
   floor with the tooth of An Angel
I imagined one night for Company in Meditation; & Pushed
   this red porphyry seat

smooth over that Mantric Rune with a Prayer to my visible &
   invisible teachers—
Beloved Stranger, Naked Beauty, terrible Eidolon O my
   youth I never dreamt that you would come."

3 am—11:30 am January 22, 1977

III

EPILOGUE

*THE ARGUMENT: Last words spoken by the bard to the boy on a
train between Washington and N.Y.*

"Some day when we surrender to each other and become One
   friend,
we'll walk back to this hermitage, returned from America
thru Cities and Bars and Smoking Factories & State Capitols
Universities, Crowds, Parks and Highways, returned from
   glass-glittering shrines
& diamond skyscrapers whose windows gleam sunset wealth
   Golden & Purple,
White & Red & Blue as Clouds that reflect Smog thru Western
   heavens.
Back here in our bodies we may renew these studies & labors
of Iron & Feather, dream copybooks, & waking Levitation of

heavy Mind.

Now still bodied separate in Vanity & minded contrary each
in's Phantasy

only Poetry's Prophetic beauty Transports us on one Train
back to households

in our north Vast City connected with telephones and buses.
We may trip out

again into Hidden Beauty, Hearts beating thru the world's
Mills & Wires, Radiant

at Television Noon or on Ecstatic midnite bed with broken
bone or body Forgetfulness.

Now we go from our Chambered Cranium forth thru Strange-
ness:

Careful to respect our Heart, mindful of Beauty's slow work-
ing Calm Machine,

Cigarette Vending Contraption or neon yellow Sun its face
to your face —

All faces different, all forms present a Face to look into with
Care:

The College boy his ignorant snub nose is a button whereon
Sexual mercies

Press their lusty thumbs & wake his studious energy. The
grey hair'd dirty

Professor of history's sought thru ages to find that Country
where Love's face is King,

While the Care on his face is King of Centuries. And thoughts
in his mind are

Presidents elected by fresh nerves every seven years to pass
new laws of Consciousness.

Each Maple waits our gaze erecting tricky branches in the
air we breathe.

Nothing is stupid but thought, & all thought we think's our
own.

My face you've seen palsied bearded White & Changing
energies

from Slavelike lust to snowy emptiness, bald Anger to fishy-
eyed prophecy,

Your voice you've heard naked and hard commanding arro-
gant, pale dandied

in a fit of Burgundy Pique, Childlike delighted fingers twist-
ing my beard

on Lion coverlets in caves far from the Iron Domed Capitol,

Intelligent deciphering runes yours and mine, dreamed &
undreamt.

Plebeian Prince of the Suburb, I return to my eastern office
pleased with our work

accident of our causes & Eidolons, Planned Careful in your
Dreams & in my daylight Frenzies: failed Projections!

Our icy wills resolved in watery black ink's translucent tears,

Love's vapors are dissolved on seaboard's clear noon open
to the Sun

shining thru railroad windows on new-revealed faces, our
own inner forms!"

January 23, 1977

I LAY LOVE ON MY KNEE

I nurs'd love where he lay
I let love get away
I let love lie low
I let my love go
I let love go along
I knew love was strong
So I let love go stray
I told love go away

I called love come home
my tongue wasn't dumb
I kissed love on the neck
& told love to come back
I told love come stay
Down by me love lay
I told love lay down
Love made a fine sound

I told love to Work
as musician or clerk
I sent love to the farm
He could do earth no harm
I told love get married
With children be harried
I said love settle down
with the worms in the ground
I told love have pity
Build me a good city

I taught love to sit
to sharpen his wit
I taught love to breathe
mindful of death
I showed love a straight spine
energetic as mine
I told love take it easy
Manners more breezy
Thoughts full of light
make love last all night

I kissed love on the brow
Where he lay like a cow
moaning and pleasured
his happy heart treasured
I kissed love's own lips
I lay love on his hips
I kissed love on his breast
When he lay down to rest
I kissed love on his thigh
Up rose his cock high

I bid Love leave me now
rest my feverish brow
I'm sick love goodbye
I must close my eye
No love you're not dead
Go find a new bed
for a day for a night

& come back for delight
after thought with new health
For all time is our wealth.

February 21, 1977

LOVE REPLIED

Love came up to me
& got down on his knee
& said I am here to serve
you what you deserve
All that you wish
as on a gold dish
eyes tongue and heart
your most private part.

Why do you eat
my behind & my feet
Why do you kiss
my belly like this
Why do you go down
& suck my cock crown

when I bare you the best
that is inside my breast

I lay there reproved
aching my prick moved
But Love kissed my ear
& said nothing to fear
Put your head on my breast
There let your skull rest
Yes hug my breast, this
is my heart you can kiss

Then Love put his face
in my tenderest place
where throbbed my breast sweet
with red hot heart's heat
There, love is our bed
There, love lay your head
There you'll never regret
all the love you can get.

From the hair to the toes
neck & knees in repose
Take the heart that I give
Give heart that you live
Forget my sweet cock
my buttock like a rock
Come up from my thighs
Hear my heart's own straight sighs

I myself am not queer
Tho I hold your heart dear
Tho I lie with you naked
tho my own heart has ached
breast to breast with your bare
body,   yes tho I dare
hug & kiss you all night
This is straight hearts' delight.

So bring your head up
from my loins or the cup
of my knees and behind
where you touch your lips blind
Put your lips to my heart
That is my public part
Hold me close and receive
All the love I can give

June 18 1977 5AM

BY ALLEN GINSBERG

Poetry Books

Howl and Other Poems. City Lights Books, 1956.
Kaddish and Other Poems. City Lights Books, 1961.
Empty Mirror, Early Poems. Totem/Corinth, 1961.
Reality Sandwiches. City Lights Books, 1963.
Ankor Wat. Fulcrum Press, 1968.
Airplane Dreams. Anansi/City Lights Books, 1968.
Planet News. City Lights Books, 1968.
The Gates of Wrath, Rhymed Poems. Four Seasons, 1972.
The Fall of America, Poems of These States. City Lights Books, 1973.
Iron Horse. Coach House Press/City Lights Books, 1974.
First Blues. Full Court Press, 1975
Sad Dust Glories, Workingman's Press, 1975.
Mind Breaths, Poems 1971-1977. City Lights Books, 1977.

Prose Books

The Yage Letters. (w/Wm. S. Burroughs), City Lights Books, 1963.
Indian Journals. David Hazelwood/City Lights Books, 1970.
Improvised Poetics. Anonym Books, 1971.
Gay Sunshine Interview. Grey Fox Press, 1974.
Allen Verbatim: Lectures on Poetry etc. McGraw Hill, 1974
The Visions of the Great Rememberer. Mulch Press, 1974.
Chicago Trial Testimony. City Lights Books, 1975.
To Eberhardt from Ginsberg. Penmaen Press, 1976.
Journals Early Fifties Early Sixties. Grove Press, 1977.
As Ever: Collected Correspondence with Neal Cassady. Creative Book Arts, 1974.

Anthologies, Interviews, Essays, Bibliographies

The New American Poetry 1945-1960. (D. Allen, ed.), Grove Press, 1960.

A Casebook of the Beat (T. Parkinson, ed.), Thomas Y. Crowell, 1961.

Paris Review Interviews (w/Tom Clark), Viking, 1967.

The Poem in Its Skin (P. Carroll, ed.) Big Table/Follett, 1968.

Playboy. (interview w/P. Carroll), 1969.

Scenes Along the Road. (Photos) (A. Charters, ed.), Gotham Book Mart, 1970.

Bibliography of the Works of Allen Ginsberg 1943-1967. (G. Dowden, ed.),City Lights Books, 1971.

Poetics of the New American Poetry. (D. Allen & W. Tallman, eds.), Grove, 1973.

The Beat Book, 1974; and *The Beat Diary*, 1977. (A. K. & G. Knight, eds.)

Loka: Journal of Naropa Institute. Anchor Doubleday, vol. 1-1975, vol. 2-1976.

The New Naked Poetry. (Berg & Mezey, eds.), Bobbs-Merrill, 1976.

Phonograph Records

Howl and Other Poems. Fantasy-Galaxy Records #7013, Berkeley, 1959.

Kaddish. Atlantic Verbum Series 4001, 1966. (op)

Wm. Blake's Songs of Innocence & of Experience tuned by A.G., MGM/Verve, 1970 (op)

Blake Album II. Fantasy-Galaxy Records, 1971 (unissued)

First Blues. John Hammond Sr., Producer (unissued)

CITY LIGHTS PUBLICATIONS

Antonin Artaud. ANTHOLOGY. $2.00

Julian Beck. THE LIFE OF THE THEATRE. $4.00

Michael Bowen. JOURNEY TO NEPAL. $2.50

Paul Bowles. A HUNDRED CAMELS IN THE COURTYARD. $1.50

Stefan Brecht. POEMS. $3.00

James Broughton. SEEING THE LIGHT. $2.50

Gov. Jerry Brown. THOUGHTS. $2.00

Charles Bukowski. ERECTIONS, EJACULATIONS, EXHIBITIONS
  AND GENERAL TALES OF ORDINARY MADNESS. $5.95

Charles Bukowski. NOTES OF A DIRTY OLD MAN. $3.50

William S. Burroughs. THE YAGE LETTERS. $2.00

Neal Cassady. THE FIRST THIRD. $3.00

CITY LIGHTS ANTHOLOGY. $5.95

CITY LIGHTS JOURNAL No. 4. $5.95

Gregory Corso. GASOLINE / THE VESTAL LADY. $2.00

Alexandra David-Neel. SECRET ORAL TEACHINGS IN TIBETAN
  BUDDHIST SECTS. $2.50

Diane diPrima. REVOLUTIONARY LETTERS. $2.50

George Dowden. BIBLIOGRAPHY OF ALLEN GINSBERG. $17.50 (cloth)

Isabelle Eberhardt. THE OBLIVION SEEKERS. $2.00

Ernest Fenollosa. THE CHINESE WRITTEN CHARACTER AS
  A MEDIUM FOR POETRY. $2.50

Lawrence Ferlinghetti. PICTURES OF THE GONE WORLD. $1.50

Lawrence Ferlinghetti. NORTHWEST ECOLOG. $2.00

Jean Genet. MAY DAY SPEECH. $1.00

Allen Ginsberg. CHICAGO TRIAL TESTIMONY. $2.00

Allen Ginsberg. THE FALL OF AMERICA. $3.00

Allen Ginsberg. HOWL & OTHER POEMS. $2.00

Allen Ginsberg. INDIAN JOURNALS. $3.00. $6.50 (cloth)

Allen Ginsberg. IRON HORSE. $3.00

Allen Ginsberg. KADDISH & OTHER POEMS. $2.50

Allen Ginsberg. MIND BREATHS. $3.50. $8.95 (cloth)

Allen Ginsberg. PLANET NEWS. $2.50

Allen Ginsberg. REALITY SANDWICHES. $1.50

Ernest Hemingway. COLLECTED POEMS. 50¢

Jack Hirschman. LYRIPOL. $2.50

James Joyce. POMES PENYEACH. $1.00

Bob Kaufman. GOLDEN SARDINE. $2.00

Jack Kerouac. BOOK OF DREAMS. $3.00

Jack Kerouac. SCATTERED POEMS. $2.00

Philip Lamantia. SELECTED POEMS. $1.50

James Laughlin. IN ANOTHER COUNTRY. $2.50. $7.50 (cloth)

Malcolm Lowry. SELECTED POEMS. $1.50

Norman Mailer. THE WHITE NEGRO. $1.00

Karl Marx. LOVE POEMS. $2.00

Henri Michaux. MISERABLE MIRACLE. $1.95

Daniel Moore. BURNT HEART. $2.50

Mohammed Mrabet. M'HASHISH. $1.50

Huey Newton & Ericka Huggins. INSIGHTS & POEMS. $2.00

Harold Norse. HOTEL NIRVANA. $2.00

Frank O'Hara. LUNCH POEMS. $2.00

Charles Olson. CALL ME ISHMAEL. $2.00

Tom Parkinson. PROTECT THE EARTH. $1.50

Kenneth Patchen. LOVE POEMS. $1.00

Kenneth Patchen. POEMS OF HUMOR & PROTEST. $1.50

Pablo Picasso. HUNK OF SKIN. $1.00

Tom Pickard. GUTTERSNIPE. $2.50

Charles Plymell. LAST OF THE MOCCASINS. $3.00

Jacques Prévert. SELECTIONS FROM PAROLES. $1.50

John Reed. ADVENTURES OF A YOUNG MAN. $3.00

Charles & Janet Richards. CHINESE COOKING. $1.50

Ed Sanders. INVESTIGATIVE POETRY. $2.00

Paul Jordan Smith. KEY TO THE ULYSSES OF JAMES JOYCE. $1.50

Gary Snyder. THE OLD WAYS. $2.50

Carl Solomon. MISHAPS PERHAPS. $1.50

Carl Solomon. MORE MISHAPS. $1.50

Italo Svevo. JAMES JOYCE $1.25

Roland Topor. PANIC. $1.00

Charles Upton. PANIC GRASS. $1.00

Andre Voznesensky. DOGALYPSE. $1.50

Anne Waldman. FAST SPEAKING WOMAN. $2.00

Arthur Waley. THE NINE SONGS. $2.50

Alan W. Watts. BEAT ZEN, SQUARE ZEN & ZEN. $1.00

Walt Whitman. AN AMERICAL PRIMER. $1.50

William Carlos Williams. KORA IN HELL: IMPROVISATIONS. $2.00

Colin Wilson. POETRY & MYSTICISM. $2.00

Pete Winslow. A DAISY IN THE MEMORY OF A SHARK. $2.00

Yevtushenko, et al. RED CATS. $1.00